Robin Klay
616-212-0486

The Smiting of the Rock
by George Palmer Putnam

Copyright © 2019 by HardPress

Address:
HardPress
8345 NW 66TH ST #2561
MIAMI FL 33166-2626
USA
Email: info@hardpress.net

KD10032

"IN AN INSTANT SHE WAS OUT OF THE SADDLE AND BENDING OVER THE PROSTRATE FIGURE." (*Page 261*)

From the drawing by Belmore Browne.

THE SMITING OF THE ROCK

A TALE OF OREGON

BY
GEORGE PALMER PUTNAM

"He smote the rock—and water came forth abundantly."
—*Numbers XX: 11.*

GROSSET & DUNLAP
PUBLISHERS   NEW YORK

COPYRIGHT, 1918
BY
G. P. PUTNAM'S SONS

Second Impression

This edition is issued under arrangement with the publishers
G. P. Putnam's Sons, New York and London

DICATED TO
L. M.

CONTENTS

CHAPTER	PAGE
I.—David Kent, Homeseeker	1
II.—A Bishop from Oregon	11
III.—Concerning Pigs	25
IV.—On the Road to Farewell	33
V.—Kent Gets a Job	42
VI.—Sunday at Little Egypt	60
VII.—Honeymoons, Perfect and Otherwise	72
VIII.—The Horse Cave	79
IX.—"Until the Resurrection"	86
X.—On Heaven and Hell	93
XI.—The Settlers' Meeting	97
XII.—Poor Little Lucy	113
XIII.—Lost Lake	120
XIV.—News Extraordinary	130
XV.—Arrival Unexpected	144
XVI.—Accident Unfortunate	156
XVII.—First Aid	168

Contents

CHAPTER	PAGE
XVIII.—A Casual Question	176
XIX.—King David's Queen	187
XX.—Pi	198
XXI.—Crete Has a Plan	207
XXII.—On the Trail, and Off	216
XXIII.—The Brain Storm	231
XXIV.—Lost and Found	252
XXV.—"Only a Draw"	257
XXVI.—Nature Takes a Hand	274
XXVII.—At the Ranger's Cabin	290
XXVIII.—The Trial	304
XXIX.—Welcome Water	313

THE SMITING OF THE ROCK

The Smiting of the Rock

CHAPTER I

DAVID KENT, HOMESEEKER

A MAY morning found David Kent gazing from his window as the train moved westward along the Oregon bank of the Columbia River. Beyond the great stream rose the rounded hills of Washington, soft as velvet in the sparkling distance. A breeze flecked the water cheerfully, mountainous snowy clouds dragged grotesque shadows across the countryside, and overhead a sunny blue sky framed the broad panorama.

The refreshing spirit of this pleasurable outlook infused the traveler, filling him with carefree content. Just then, if Chance had sought to make capital of his optimistic good nature he might have been bent to almost any purpose. But Chance left him so undisturbedly drinking in the visual magnificence of the Columbia country that shortly he was satiated with the very glory of it, and sought something less overwhelming to look upon.

The Smiting of the Rock

From his pocket he extracted a much-handled map, and spreading it out upon his knees, for the twentieth time delved into its allurements.

It was a normal folder, with the United States ironed out encouragingly and so fashioned that the red-printed route of the railroad whose name it bore was by all odds the straightest and shortest between the two oceans. Railroad map makers, he mused, long since discarded the copybook axiom that a straight line is the shortest distance between two points, substituting therefor the ukase that their own roads must always appear as the shortest, whatever their actual indirections.

What most interested Kent, however, was not the ingenious alignment of the great transcontinental, but a blank space as large as his palm, right there in Oregon, across whose threshold he had just come. Not a single railroad appeared in this typeless barren. Nowhere on the entire map could he find another neglected area nearly so large as this one into which a plain-faced Bishop, a superlatively pretty girl, and a hasty resolution were thrusting him.

A dot in the middle of the white space bore the title "Farewell Ford," and had for companions two isolated lines of letters, one spelling "Desert" and the other "Timber."

The young man's finger traced the route he was then following along the Columbia, whence a stubby half-inch of railroad reached south toward

Farewell Ford, ending just within the radius of the barren void at a dot inscribed "Shaniko."

"Goin' in?" asked the conductor.

"In where?"

"Oh, it's new to you, eh? I meant up yonder." An official thumb indicated regions behind the hills. "Know that country pretty well. How far you goin'?"

Kent indicated his ticket.

"Sure, I know it *reads* Shaniko, but no one stops there unless it's a case of sudden death."

The traveler laughed.

"Is it as bad as that?"

"Yep. Fact is, there's only one place worse'n Shaniko, which is Biggs, and here we are now."

And forthwith the Easterner, still pondering this cheering recommendation of Biggs, was deposited in its midst together with a mail sack and his own trunk. Sitting on the latter, he leisurely took stock of the surroundings as the train deserted him.

Between the tracks and cliffs which tumbled down nearly to the water's edge, was Biggs itself, nestling hotly among soiled, ruffled dunes of sand.

Single story buildings occupied one side of the lonesome street, whose corrugated drifts attested its innocence of traffic. At each end of the "block" was a saloon, efficiently located so that it was impossible to come or go without running temptation's gauntlet. Before a hotel of unpainted lumber occupying the center of the line, a white-aproned individual ding-donged a brazen triangle by way of urging the public to eat. And there were several erstwhile pretentious structures with lofty and deceitful clapboard pompadours, bearing faded inscriptions of dealers in other people's real estate. Bottles, cans, and sundry souvenirs of hungers and thirsts long since satisfied fringed the human habitations.

"Must get hot in summer," Kent ventured to the agent, who came for the mail pouch.

"Yep. A hundred an' ten most of the time. But it's better'n *that*,"—accurately winging a congealed eddy with an excess of tobacco juice,— "the sand makes most trouble. When it breezes a bit, you've gotter wear goggles, and when she honest-ter-God *blows* you've just gotter *quit*."

On the way to the eating place, which he unblushingly recommended, the agent recounted how a few "reg'lar" sandstorms would cut down telephone posts, by the incessant drive of the sharp particles against the wood.

Shortly, the two-car train rattled in from behind the hills and by the time it was headed around on the "Y" the limited from the West, emerging from a cloud of dust on the main line, stopped, deposited a handful of passengers, and again sped on its way. The human deposit included two drummers, a rancher, an individual with a glass eye, and a young lady. The four men sprinted to the food dispensary, where one of the drummers, greeting the proprietor with cordial profanity, hoped that "Charley wouldn't pull out till they stowed some hash."

"Charley," who was the conductor of the Shaniko train, showed more gallantry than the herd at the trough.

"Beg pardon, Miss, but there's ten minutes to get a bite to eat, if you wish."

The lone young lady, so addressed, assured Charley that she would go without. "I'm not hungry," she added, smiling thanks for his interest.

Kent, overhearing, all at once felt sure that it was not lack of appetite but disinclination to brave the rigors of the eating house that kept the girl from luncheon. So forthwith he found himself exchanging cash for jet coffee in a cup and megalithic ham sandwiches in a flyspecked paper bag.

"Waste of time, my frien'," proffered a fishy-eyed drummer between mouthfuls. "She won't thaw. I've tried."

Despite the pessimistic counsel, the young man plowed back through the sand to the depot, to find that the girl was already on the Shaniko train. So he climbed aboard, balancing the coffee, now rather worse than lukewarm, and commencing to feel foolishly self-conscious after the fashion of mankind detected in chivalry.

"I beg your pardon, but . . . won't you please take these?" He was standing in front of her. "I thought you were . . . hm . . . that is, of course, you couldn't go up to that hole so I took the liberty of . . . " his embarrassment got the better of him, and further words balked.

There is no slightest doubt that if the worldly drummer had laid a luxurious repast upon the altar of acquaintanceship, the result would have been disaster—to the drummer. But Kent's worldliness was somehow of a different world. The blue eyes appraised the knight of the coffee cup evenly. Evidently they were satisfied with what they saw, as forthwith the drummer who said there was no thawing was proved a liar.

"It's good of you. I really might have starved to death."

There was no affectation in that spontaneous smile with its array of white teeth, and Kent, who hitherto had noticed next to nothing about the girl, found himself wondering if perhaps her "curly" upper lip might be a trifle too short. Certainly her teeth were square and firm, for a woman; and her chin, that too——

"How can we get the cup back?" The coffee gone, the housewifely problem at once struck her.

"Throw it away! It's paid for."

"Which reminds me—how much was it all?"

"Nothing. You see they gave it to me!"

But the fib availed not at all against the insistence of the blue-eyed girl who had no slightest intention of permitting chance young men—even if they were respectful—to pay for her meals. Finally he said, "A quarter."

"Two bits," she corrected, and forced his acceptance of the coin. "Thank you, again."

With that she began to study the country, and Kent took the hint. Looking back from the smoking car the drummer grinned and went through the pantomime of shaking his own hand in congratulation.

"Dirty beast," thought Kent, and succeeded in concentrating most of his attention on the landscape.

For an hour the diminutive train panted up oppressive grades, the track meandering through crooked canyons and along gullies where winter rain had washed away the adobe, leaving brick-colored chasms and piles of rounded rock. Stunted sagebrush and chemise clothed the hillsides scantily, and trails of cattle serried every slope, as evenly as the contour lines on a map. Then, the rim of the Columbia's hills reached, the train rattled southward with more directness and some pretense of speed, across a rolling plateau of stubblefields, golden with wheat at harvest time, but at that season richly toned with browns and wakening green. Ranch houses and little towns alone broke the pleasant monotony of the wide country. Beyond the drab foreground and the blue haziness of the middle distance, the Cascade mountains silhouetted against the western sky, with Mount Hood, cloaked in the white of everlasting snow, marshaling an array of lesser peaks.

As the afternoon wore on Kent devoted himself to a cumulative letter which had commenced east of Chicago and was to be mailed nowhere short of Oregon. The autobiographic narrative reached Biggs and the hungry girl simultaneously, and somehow there hung fire.

Consideration of that incident brought a smile to the idling author. Could one imagine *his* lady accepting provender from a total stranger? One could not. As a matter of fact, the very idea of aristocratic Valentine being either unescorted or hungry was untenable. So, dismissing the unlikely comparison from his mind, for lack of better ammunition he tore the map from the folder, sketched himself racing across the fruitless barren toward Farewell Ford, and placed his artistic effort with the corpulent letter in an envelope.

Looking up from his accomplished task, Kent's eyes encountered those of the erstwhile hungry girl, unexpectedly enough to surprise an amused twinkle. Immediately the observer's eyes retreated to her magazine, leaving Kent resentfully aware that he was blushing unreasonably.

As they neared Shaniko the drummers, with the hope of making up an automobile load, inquired his destination.

"Farewell. But let's leave plans until we get there." Having no alternative, they agreed.

"Will you go through to-night?"

The girl's question followed the exit of the drummers.

"I really don't know. You see, it's all new to me. What does one do, anyway?"

"There's the choice of stage or automobile," she replied. "The autos are new on the run, and of course cost more. The stage starts to-night, and the auto leaves in the morning. Both of them get to Farewell about the same time to-morrow evening."

"It's a case of riding all night on the stage, then?"

"Oh, yes. It's really not as bad as it sounds— quite fun, in fact, if you like that sort of thing." She was talking very easily now.

"*You* do, I suppose." He had hit upon the shade of her eyes—cornflower blue.

"Yes, I really do, in a way," she seemed to ponder the matter. "And then this is the longest stage ride left, I believe, and it's somehow rather bully to get this last taste of what used to be everywhere in the West. But, of course, it's awfully tiring, and the dust is getting bad again now."

Dust! That was it; gold with dust over it— the very fittest description of her hair, thought Kent, who had a habit of wording ideas.

"I'm going to Farewell, too," the girl continued. "The auto fare is twenty dollars and the stage ten, so of course I go by stage."

"Of course," Kent's echo quite surprised him.

When the girl spoke of the auto he had decided on it quite automatically. Now, however, the unaccustomed consideration of cost was leveled full in his face by a young lady who made nothing heroic of choosing an all-night ride in preference to a ten-dollar extravagance.

"Money is very scarce in a new country," the girl offered.

"And other places, too. The auto fare does seem horribly high . . . quite out of sight for a poor"—he fumbled for a word, and found one—"homeseeker. The stage for me—of course."

For the remainder of the journey the volunteer homeseeker furtively clasped the letter he had written while his mind wandered far away whither that letter was to go.

CHAPTER II

A BISHOP FROM OREGON

IN retrospect, as the train bore him nearer Shaniko, David Kent recalled the events which had embarked him on his present quest. The commencement of it all, he remembered well, dated from a dinner at the home of Mrs. Alton Pennoyer, mother of the girl to whom his first Oregon letter had just been addressed.

But behind that dinner, and as such the actual key to the entire adventure, lay a newspaper article which had signaled the social unearthing, or at least rehabilitation, of a certain missionary Prelate of the West.

"OREGON BISHOP BACK FROM FRONTIER THRILLS NEW YORK AUDIENCE"

was the heading which caught the attention of Mrs. Pennoyer as she glanced through her paper one April morning.

"The address of the Right Rev. Robert Rudd, Bishop of Eastern Oregon, was the principal feature of yesterday's session of the National

Settlement Workers Association. Bishop Rudd, who at one time was himself prominent in local settlement activity, has for several years been engaged in what is practically missionary work in a far western territory aptly described by him as 'the largest railroadless area in the United States.' With his strong personality, unique experiences, and decidedly advanced theories, this militant worker from the West created something of a furore."

Mrs. Pennoyer read no further. That first paragraph was enough. For she had known Robert Rudd's "people," and the Bishop of to-day, in the yesterday of knickerbockers, had more than once encountered her disapproval with his full-blooded pranks.

"Val, do you remember Robert Rudd?" said Mrs. Pennoyer to her daughter, whose entrance coincided with the enveloping of a note to Rudd himself.

It required close to six seconds of concentration—which became her very prettily—for Valentine to rescue the memory of Bob Rudd from a brain stocked with recollections of many males.

"Yes, Mummsie, I remember—quite well. He was awfully ugly and awfully nice. What about him?"

"He is a Bishop now."

And Mrs. Pennoyer, handing her daughter the envelope which she had just addressed, explained that she was asking the Bishop to dinner, which surprised Valentine not at all as her mother was constantly on the alert for itinerant lions who might be induced to roar acceptably as her guests.

"You are going out, I see, so please mail it. And Val,—" Mrs. Pennoyer's hesitancy betrayed her half-certainty of the answer even before she put the question,"—where are you going?"

"Oh, just *out!*"

"My dear—," Mrs. Pennoyer cleared her throat. "My dear—" then, rather lamely "—please sit down."

Being a young lady of decision, Valentine took the conversational bull by the horns.

"Please, Mummsie, listen. You're right. I am going walking with Mr. Kent. I think I like him very much, but I haven't the least idea of marrying him."

"Girls never have." The abrupt onslaught left Mrs. Pennoyer just enough breath and brains to slip that in—it was the very best she could do. Valentine laughed, all at once quite enjoying the shift of affairs. Spurred by spring morn madness, she raced on.

"If you're anxious for the news, Da—that is, Mr. Kent wants to marry me, and I told him . . . " a dramatic pause evidenced Valentine's appreciation of the value of suspense ". . . that I would let him know . . . after a while."

Again a halt.

"So this morning I am going to give him my decision—isn't it mean, Mummsie, that there is always something to be decided? I loathe decisions." Pause number three. "Shall I tell you?"

Mrs. Pennoyer gasped, but contrived to nod.

"Well, Mummsie, I am not going to marry him . . . yet!"

The corners of the mother's mouth trembled.

"Listen, Mummsie." Now, it was the little girl recounting her troubles, and no longer the clever débutante playing hide-and-go-seek with a distressed parent. "There really isn't anything to tell. I like David—a lot. But I haven't the slightest idea whether I really love him. I know you and Dads don't approve and . . ."

"Not that either, my dear," her mother interrupted. "We like Mr. Kent well enough. I am sure he is a very worthy young man. . . ."

"Well, then, it's money. Oh, yes it is! No use pretending. He's acceptable as a guest, but you'd not urge him as a son-in-law. I know. Haven't I heard Dads thresh it all out? 'A pleasant fellow, but one who doesn't seem to get anywhere,' is the way Dads catalogues him. 'My only daughter must marry a leader, a man who *does* things.' Oh glory, I know it by heart! Jerry Whitemore is eligible; he's 'successful'— a broker—what David calls a gentleman gambler. Then there's that little peanut Forsythe: a born diplomat, Dads calls him, and perhaps it's true he can't help being a big Ambassador or something-or-other some day. Imagine Mrs. Gail Forsythe——" She pursed her lips tastefully over the experimental phrase.

"His family, Valentine——"

"Lordy, yes, I know! it's older than a Swiss cheese, and no member of the illustrious tribe ever did anything to be ashamed of since leaving the Ark, unless you count marrying for money!"

The conversation just then was punctuated by the discreet cough of the superbly discreet butler bearing the card of Mr. David Kent.

Valentine ordained she would "be there in a minute," and then took five rearranging details of her personal appearance, which, judging from its nicety, seemingly already had been brought to a state of perfection.

Completing her leisurely devotions at the shrine of beauty, she abandoned the mirror, regained her gloves and the Bishop's invitation, and smiled like a sunrise.

"Don't worry, Mummsie. Remember, I am practical." With that enigmatical farewell, Youth sought waiting Man, leaving Middle Age sighing concernedly.

"Well, I'll do what I want anyway." The daughter unburdened herself of this very probable axiom as she approached the library and her suitor. "Only what do I want to do?"

The plan to make Bishop Rudd the social *pièce de résistance* of a considerable gathering did not materialize, for the answer to Mrs. Pennoyer's invitation was politely determined in its regretfulness. Acceptance was impossible, it appeared, because the Bishop was to deliver an address upon the opportunities of the West before a remote organization of which his would-be hostess had never heard.

The upshot was that Bishop Robert Rudd and David Kent were the sole guests at what their hostess called a "simple family dinner," which, to accommodate the Bishop's appointment, commenced and ended early.

At the outset of the meal Mrs. Pennoyer personally conducted the conversation, drawing from her guest tales of his frontier experiences. But while the Bishop's reminiscences came freely enough, the personal element in them was disappointingly subdued. It was not of himself and his deeds which he cared to talk, but of the big half-tamed country where his work held him. Of that, and its people, he enthused with heartfelt warmth.

"That's all extremely interesting, Bishop, but honestly now," Miss Pennoyer smiled dazzlingly, "wouldn't it be nicer back here where things are . . . well, where everything is more comfortable . . . and cultured?"

The exponent of Western enthusiasm regarded her gravely.

"I dare say it would be *nicer*," he replied dryly.

"But Bishop," Kent sought to give the conversation a safer turn, "do you really believe that West of yours is a better country than this?"

"No . . . it's worse!"

"Is that why you like it?" Kent laughed.

"Or is it the necessity of reforming it that appeals to you?" added Miss Pennoyer.

"Neither . . . and both. I went out there prejudiced against the West and I've come back prejudiced in its favor. It's a very virulent disease, this love of the country, I assure you . . . and highly contagious. So far as reforming goes, I hope to Heaven it may never be reformed . . . there's lots more need for reformation right here in New York. Anyway," he chuckled at some recollection, "the only really sophisticated sinning we have is imported . . . by Easterners! Where there's plently of out-of-doors and sky and mountains the misdeeds of men aren't very reprehensible. They're apt to be primal and rather clean and big . . . almost commendable, if you know what I mean."

Kent thought he knew. In fact, the more he heard this Bishop talk—and his outlook on life seemed extraordinarily unbishoply—the more warmly rekindled his old admiration, taking him back to the time when he, a schoolboy, had idolized Rudd, the college man, heroically returning home between terms. By the time dinner was over, a half resolve had formed in the young man's mind.

Shortly, and somewhat to his own surprise, Kent was unburdening himself to the Bishop. He was dissatisfied with his life, its idleness and lack of purpose. He wanted to make good, to do something on his own initiative, somehow, somewhere. That he made clear, and intentionally. He also made reasonably clear, although without intention, that some compelling reason had lately arisen for this new and creditable resolve. And the Bishop, in his wisdom, and glancing casually in the direction of Valentine Pennoyer, gleaned a far better comprehension of the situation than his companion imagined.

"Your trouble, old chap, is that you've been boiling long enough . . . you need to jell now," said the Bishop.

"Jell?"

"Exactly. Ever see a New England cook make jelly? Remember what fine firm material comes from the restless mass in the kettle . . . after it's boiled enough and got a chance to settle down?"

Kent laughed aloud.

"Jell . . . that's just the word! I need to jell. But do you suppose I've been on the stove too long?"

The Bishop eyed him squarely. "No," said he.

"Long enough?"

"That's hard to say. Each brand requires a different recipe. Possibly you'd better stew for a time at a lower temperature, or have some new ingredients added."

"Or try a new stove?"

A Bishop from Oregon 19

"Perhaps. However, my observation is that it's the cook which counts most . . . a good cook can get results anywhere. And of course you realize"—the little Bishop's deep-set eyes twinkled behind their thick lenses—"that girls make the best cooks!"

Just then Miss Pennoyer joined them.

"What is all this confab?" she asked.

"We've been discussing cooking . . . and cooks."

"A deadly dull text, I'm sure."

"We were especially concerned with jelly," he added, to her further mystification. "Don't you find men who have 'jelled' the most worth while?"

But Miss Pennoyer was spared the exertion of further progress along this conversational byway through the advent of her mother, who sallied forth into the outer hall, where they stood, to speed the parting guest with additional farewell.

"And David," the Bishop shook Kent's hand as they parted on the steps, "if you do want to try transplanting for a while, remember, Oregon's the place. You'd never regret it."

The little Bishop swung off down the sidewalk to his meeting of lowly young men concerned with occidental opportunities, and David Kent returned to the sumptuous Pennoyer drawing-room, with a plan formulating within him.

"If I make good will that settle the matter?" he said to Valentine later.

"Oh, David, don't be silly! Things like . . . like getting married aren't settled that way. . . ."

"Well, how is it done, then?" He took her two hands in his, forcing her to regard him, and the issue, squarely. "You said only yesterday you loved me and the only reason you'd not promise was because I didn't seem to be steady . . . to know what I meant to do. And your father . . . oh yes, I know all about that—" he smothered her protest—" he throws a fit on the floor whenever I'm considered as a possible son-in-law. Now, isn't that true?"

She nodded, with a challenging smile. It was true enough, and she knew it.

"Dads won't have me marry a failure . . . and I don't want to. I'd . . . like to have you succeed, David."

"That's very businesslike and practical," he replied good-humoredly. "You see, Val, I don't blame your father . . . at least I won't hold it against him! And while it's inconvenient, it's reasonable enough for you to want me to try my hand at something beside spending my modest income. So I've a business proposition to make to you . . . it's a bit out of the ordinary and entirely unromantic, I suppose."

"Well?" said she.

If Valentine Pennoyer had been a shade less beautiful, and the spell she had cast over David Kent a shade less irresistible, the coolly selfish, passionless poise of her might well have shattered his quixotic notions and the yearning warmth beneath them. But the young man was too much in love for critical appraisement.

"Bishop Rudd made a great hit with me . . . also Oregon, as he describes it. Right now, I suppose, he's telling about those 'opportunities for young men' out there. Well, Val, I'm one of the young men who intends starting a still hunt for success out Oregon way, provided only"— he paused, impressively—"it's distinctly worth while."

"How about me?" Valentine's words echoed her first thought.

"That's just the point. You're the beginning and the end of it all. I'm going out there to show you I can make good. And if I do," this time he loosed one hand to raise her chin so he could look into her eyes, "will you promise to marry me?"

"Making good," she parried, "is so much a matter of comparisons."

"All right, then. I'll leave the deciding to you . . . and your practical father. And no promises asked. Only I'll tell you what I'm going to do. Just as soon as possible I start for that country the Bishop raves about. . . . Farewell's the name of the town. I'll need some steers from him as to how to get there, and aside from that I'll not discuss the matter with a soul. I won't even take any money . . . just enough to land me there. What else I have I'll tuck away where it won't be touched. We're to play this little game for a year, Val . . . does that suit?"

"You mean you'll stay away a year? Oh, David! . . ."

"Not necessarily. But I'm going to put in twelve months absolutely on my own resources. I'll start on the dead level when I get out there . . . broke. I may be still broke when the year's over but at least I'll manage to get through it and show your estimable parent I can support myself."

Valentine smiled as he unfolded his plan. And beneath the smile was a sense of genuine satisfaction. The novelty, the unique practicability of it, pleased her.

"No cheating?" she chided.

"None. The game's to be played square. And, Val . . . I thought first I'd ask you to make a bargain . . . a promise. Perhaps that wouldn't be fair. But if this is to be an honest-to-goodness business deal, why, I ought to have . . . well, say an option."

"What's that? . . . it sounds depressingly legal."

"It's a sort of testimonial of prior right, I guess. The idea is that Oregon is a long way off . . ."

"You chose it, not I!"

"True enough. But even at that, Val, I'm going into this party for you . . . to get you anyway . . . and it's only fair my . . . ahem

... rights should be protected in my absence. I don't want ... well, you shouldn't allow any poaching."

"So that's it! Shall I hang a 'No Trespassing' sign around my neck?"

He assured her it would be an excellent idea.

"David, dear," she announced finally, "it strikes me there is a lot of nonsense about all this ... it's sort of ... well, storybookish and fanciful." She frowned. Romancing held little appeal for this modern princess.

"And yet," she continued, "it's really commonsense and reasonable. It's quite true, David, that Dads doesn't enthuse over you as a do-nothing. He's always been a doer himself, and a successful one, and it's natural he'd have little respect for a man who has never ... well, never made his own way."

"And you precious near share the paternal viewpoint," put in the subject of the appraisement, ruefully.

"Yes, to a degree ... but fortunately"—a delighting smile replaced her thoughtful look—"fortunately I think somewhat more of you than Dads does ... fortunately for you, at least. But I want you to succeed, David ... you must succeed. ... No, keep away, please! .. you haven't made good yet, remember ... and I *do* like this idea of yours, even with all its foolishness ... it's so much better than working around in a circle, the way we've been doing for so long now. As the Bishop says, it will give you a chance to find yourself . . . and it ought to let me find out what I really want, too. Of course it's a gamble. . . ."

"Call it a flier in success," he interjected.

"Or failure. Anyway, Dads says even a good business man takes a flier now and then. So I'll take this one, David. Yes, I'll agree to keep footfree until the end of the year. I'll try not even to run risks of getting engaged. And you're to live up to the rules of the game too . . . go out there all on your own hook and sink or swim without calling for help. That's a bargain."

"Honesttogod" said Kent.

They shook hands quite solemnly. But instead of releasing her hand in a businesslike manner, the male party to this quixotic contract drew the party of the second part to him, abruptly and strongly, while the seal was affixed.

CHAPTER III

CONCERNING PIGS

At the Shaniko hotel a chemically-blonded waitress bawled orders for beans, ham, and coffee into an aperture at one end of the dining-room, whence in time issued the culinary products accompanied by a fragrance not exclusively their own. The drummers consumed their supper loudly. The girl of the train was at another table, conversing with an eager little man, whom she had affectionately greeted as "Dad." In the tooth-picking lull, following pie, when everyone backed up against the stove in the lobby, Kent gleaned from the clerk that the little man's name was Trumble.

"Miss Trumble, eh? At least I know someone at Farewell," he thought.

It was the same "Dad" who held the reins when they climbed into the stage, the girl tucked beside him, while Kent shared the inside with a horse buyer who speedily exhausted the contents of a pint bottle without any apparent effects, ill or otherwise.

During the cold night Kent slept scarcely at all,

although his companion, to judge by his snoring, contrived considerable slumber. Another member of the party contributed also to the night revels. This one was a small pig traveling in a crate fastened in the rear beside Kent's trunk, sundry boxes of California fruit, and other variegated cargo.

Finally, the mud and rocks of Shaniko Flats and the steep grades of Cow Canyon were negotiated, and about two o'clock the stage stopped.

"What's matter?" The horse buyer lurched into wakefulness, automatically reaching to make sure his glass eye was in place.

"Nothin' special, 'cept breakfast. This is Heisler's." The little driver's lantern illuminated the after end of his craft with a glow more dim than religious, whereat the pig resumed his squealing. "How's all the live stock riding?" The query was addressed indiscriminately in the direction of pig and passengers.

The two men got out stiffly and the girl, swinging down from her seat, wished them a good morning.

A lantern appeared from somewhere, a couple of shadow men led the horses off, and the lower windows of a house close at hand showed golden squares of light.

"Hello, Dad!" a woman's voice called. "Back at it, eh?"

"Yu betcha. S'like old times." The driver's cheery voice warmed the arctic night. All at once hot coffee and a stove seemed possible attainments and not mirages of the roadside.

"Don't forget to water the pig, Dad," the girl reminded, as she went to the house.

"Ain't that just like her—never forgets nothing"; the driver's friendly voice was full of admiration. "Well, suppose it's gotter be done—the bygod pig's paying first-class fare 'n must be 'tended." With a sigh of good-natured protest, Trumble, placing the lantern on the ground, fumbled with the stiff cords binding the crate while Kent and his fellow passenger stamped some semblance of warmth into their feet.

"Hey, one of you, help me here—quick!"

But succor came too late. In the dark something slipped and with a clatter trunk, fruit boxes, and crate tumbled over, extinguishing the lantern and knocking Trumble into the dust, whence a remarkable offering of diversified profanity ascended. The light crate splintered as it hit the road, and the panicky porker scuttled away into the blackness.

A door opened and the girl's voice floated through the night.

"What *is* the matter?"

The swearing subsided.

"Nothin'. Oh, nothin' *at all*." Withering sarcasm was in that announcement. "'Ceptin' only"—a laborious grunt as the little man gathered himself up—"a half ton lit square on top o' me an' I'm . . . all . . . busted . . . up." The last words came with the deliberation of excessive suffering.

"Not really hurt, Dad?" She had hurried to his side through the blackness, and spoke with tender concern.

"No—o, reckon I ain't . . . ain't *dead*, anyway." The admission came begrudgingly. "But I *might* ha' been."

The girl laughed, and the little man, his persistent good humor restored, joined her, while Kent chorused in heartily. But gloom returned as Trumble remembered the pig.

"Th' bygod pig's lit out. Well, we'll have to catch 'im if it takes all night, he bein' so special. Discoverin' pigs in the dark is some entertainin'."

The experience justified the description. With two lanterns commandeered from the barn the quest commenced. The shadows and nooks along the picket fence were searched, and every lurking-place behind sagebrush or rock became a center of investigation. But no pig.

"Well, it's tough. Humsoever, what must be can't be helped. In the mornin'," this to the native volunteer, "you'll find the beggar,—a likely lookin' young boar. Now just slip down to the barn with me an' we'll find a twin brother to stick in this bygod crate. What th' honor'ble Sprunk'd do himself is none too bad for me . . . and beside, we don't particularly delight in playin' hide an' go seek in the dark with any of Jim Failing's stray property."

Concerning Pigs 29

Trumble and the grinning boy were starting for the barn when an ill-advised squeak in the shadow directly beneath the stage disclosed the whereabouts of his porkship, devouring California fruit with evident relish.

"Ain't that just what you'd expect o' Failing?" Yanking out the offending pig by a hind foot, the little man proceeded to lay its perversity at its owner's door. "An' expensive fruit, too. Well, th' hon'ble Jim'll have ter pay."

"Who's this blackguard Failing?" Kent asked laughingly.

"How'd you know he was a black'ard?" Trumble's attitude displayed suspicion mingled with pleased anticipation. "Do they know it on the *outside?*"

"Great Scott, no." Kent hastened to withdraw from deepening water. "I don't even know who the man is—just gathered you're not fond of him. And of course any pig who'll be as mean as this one shows the effects of contaminating influence."

The girl laughed, but the little driver clearly was disappointed.

A half hour later, when the edges of appetites were turned, Kent came back to the pig episode.

"Who's Failing—if it's a fair question?"

"Puffec'ly fair. He's the meanest man in Oregon—and there's heaps o' competition." More definite information from the girl established

James Failing as Manager of the Bonanza Irrigation Company, with headquarters at Farewell.

"Who's your friend Sprunk—the fellow you intimated exchanged pigs?—what I really need is a 'Who's Who in Central Oregon'!"

"I don't intimate at all with Sprunk. He's no frien' o' mine." Trumble's reply was chilly. However, the girl came to the rescue.

"Oh, Dad, please tell him the judge's hog story. You see," this to Kent, "Mr. Sprunk is judge of the county. It's because he and Mr. Failing are cronies that Dad dislikes him."

"Well, sir, it's like this," commenced the stage driver after appropriate urging. "This here Judge Sprunk's a Democrat, but of course in these days t'aint right ter hold *that* agin him—not unreasonable, anyway. It's just last year he landed in office, after about six tries, an' then he only made the grade on a flivver. This here hog indigent happened afore he was judge—jes an onery officeseeker. Sprunk always was ace high on stock raisin' and went hard after the blue ribbons at the county fair, but somehow he never scored much in the hog line, which riled him, because he's about as conceited as he's onery. So he sent to the outside for a full blood Polin Chiny boar. Well, th' bygod boar got to Shaniko all right. I was there myself when he arove."

Trumble's ruddy cheeks quaked with laughter at the recollection.

"It was a dirty trick—quite *dis*graceful, sir."

The twinkle in the blue eyes belied the heavy tragedy air of the confession. "It happened same's to-night, only up at Shaniko; the blame boar got away. We went over the town with a fine tooth comb but never found him. Well, sir, that there piece o' pork had kum clear from Ioway by express an' was all kinds of a high roller with a reg'lar bygod family tree and all them trimmin's. If Sprunk got just an empty crate, it'd break him all up, not ter mention us boys what with damages to pay. So nacherly, we turned to, roped a scummy runt of a boar with no more pedigree than a coyote, back of Frenchy Estebenet's saloon, and tacked him up neat and sweet in that lovely empty crate. An' at that he didn't look much different from number one."

"Was Mr. Sprunk pleased?" Kent inquired.

"Never asked him. His receipt was all I wanted." The speaker devoted a minute's attention to pie. "Well, sir, we'd most forgotten about Sprunk's boar until two seasons later th' sequel o' the story, as they say, sort o' oozed out at the county fair. Sprunk was strong on hogs that season, and had a pen full o' Polin Chinys that'd put your eye out. That breed, yer know, has a considerable pepperin' of black spots down the back, and Sprunk's were spotted to the queen's taste. When the judges came along there was nothin' to it; those Polin Chinys showed up exagly by the book, and the blue ribbons was slapped on 'em immediate. But I reckon the Lord must have been lookin' an' felt sort o' sad for the other hogs, for all ter wonct he opened up a tarnation big thunder shower right over the fair grounds."

"What's that got to do with the Judge's hogs?" Kent asked.

"Oh, jus' that *stove blackin' nacherly will run when it gets wet !* An' by the time Sprunk came to rescue his bygod pets, half th' folks in the county was crowding around th' pen in the rain watchin' the black splotches wash clean on them Polin Chinys an' laughin' their heads off. Sprunk kinder retired for a while after that, altho' he did talk o' suing the stage company for libel or arson or somethin'."

The story teller lit his pipe.

"Well, girls an' boys, it's mos' three o'clock. Le's pretend we've had a night's sleep an' keep going."

CHAPTER IV

ON THE ROAD TO FAREWELL

DAYLIGHT came, a third relay of bony nags took their places at Shallow Creek, and as the sun thawed the travelers, the road climbed over the broad back of Bear Mountain and down its pine-covered southern flanks. Again they emerged into lowlands, where occasional fields were interspersed among the sagebrush flats, and shortly after noon reached Roundville, in the wide bottom where the creeks of Alamo and McCree join Winding River.

Thirty-five miles westward lay Farewell Ford, half the distance another climb from the valley to the shoulder of Long Butte, whence the watershed of Welcome River sloped westerly. Beyond the river, on whose banks nestled Farewell, the timbered foothills of the Cascades clamber upward and westward, merging into the mountains whose snowy summits form a barrier dividing the semi-arid hinterland of Central Oregon from the Willamette Valley and the damp coastal regions.

The afternoon was waning when the stage gained

the summit of the last divide, and by mutual consent of driver and driven came to a standstill in the shade of a gnarled juniper tree.

Where a fringe of dark green marked the edge of the timber a single hill stood out in the plain, like a sentinel guarding the approach to its fellows.

"Over yonder's Farewell, just at the foot of the butte." The driver indicated the solitary cone. "In the old days immigrants headin' for the Ford steered by it, so it come to be called th' Pilot. We always feel sorter better when we see it agin—'s like gettin' home."

"And true enough, there's no place quite so good—as home," the girl added.

"Be it ever so humble," Kent offered, smilingly.

"The right word, I fear." There was pathos in the girl's answering smile as her eyes wandered over the familiar solitudes of her brown homeland. "It's all pretty humble, isn't it, Dad?"

"Humble? Why, *that's* too purty a name." Old man Trumble admonished Kent with a stubby forefinger. "It's dirt ter admit it, but this here's the godawfulest country that ever slipped by the Creator. There's humbleness same as in all new countries, only here we've got humbug beside."

"Why, Dad, you're a *knocker*." Real reproach was in the words. To admit that one's chosen land falls short of perfection is to play traitor in a region where flagrant optimism is religion.

"No such thing." The pessimist defended

himself with the self-certainty of positive innocence. "It's only a little truth leaking through the chinks of righteousness—this here sunlight opens 'em up. Jus' take them little books th' company puts out, chock-ablock with nifty pictures. You can read all about this garden of Eden an' how water's all that's needed to make it blossom like the rose and more highfalutin' stuff of the same brand." Despite his indignant words, even a stranger could guess that deep down in his heart the little driver half believed it all was actually as desirable as Eden. "The country might be worse, but it doesn't get no show with a nest of bunco artists milking it and the settlers dry. Why, this gal here——"

"Hush, Dad," the "gal" interrupted.

"Won't! It's gospel, an' he might as well hear now as later," he insisted. "She's just back from the State capital down ter Salem. Tried to get the Land Board to understan' what's going on in here—how they're selling land before they're able to deliver water and then selling more to pay for getting it to the first afore the settlers starve to death. Why, sir, it's—it's a crime!" The little man's blazing indignation sank suddenly as if oppressed by the hopelessness of the case. There was no fire left as he continued. "Last year dozens of ranchers who'd cleared land and even put crops in never got a drop of water, so's their whole season's work went for nothin'!"

"Didn't they complain?" Kent asked.

"Complain? Yu betcha! One of 'em got throwed out of Failing's office—took a piece of the door with him—he complained so hard. Yes, they got th' State officials in, too, but that just meant rides around in ortermobiles, a luncheon an' booze with Failing, and what they advertised as a 'settlers' meeting' where no one had a chance to speak 'cept friends o' the company. Oh, it's rotten enough!

"It's the same old fight for a living of the first ones in a new country." The driver pursued his vein of thought. "I've seen it a dozen times this side of the Missouri. It's a hard country, but it'll come out all right in th' end." He took up the reins. "But say," there was a gleam in the old blue eyes and a tightening of the wrinkles about them, "I wouldn't swap it for any country in this little old world—nor'd you, after six months."

The young Easterner smiled. The words brought to his mind the picture of a dinner in New York, where another loyal enthusiast had defended the reputation of this adverse country with positive affection—and a tall, gray-clad girl had listened as to a voice from strange lands, not entirely comprehensible.

"Why, that's exactly what Bishop Rudd says."

"Sufferin' cats! Do you know the Bish? You do, eh? Well, if that ain't the bygodest luck." The little driver exuded pleasure.

"You see, the Bishop is a special friend of ours," the girl explained. "Dad here swears by him—and *at* most other people, as perhaps you've noticed!"

After they had heard what seemed best of Kent's acquaintanceship with Rudd and of the New York meeting which started his feet on the road to Farewell Ford, the stage rolled on towards Welcome River with a fine air of briskness.

The young man rode with only his thoughts for company, the horse buyer having remained at Roundville, and dust-framed glimpses of silvery juniper trees, sagebrush, and brown earth as a background for his mental excursioning. Despite the first blush of barrenness which the land of his self-made adventure presented, Kent was superbly satisfied. New York seemed a part of another world (which indeed it was), and he was all at once shocked in realizing that the intimate personal element had somehow gone from his consideration of Valentine Pennoyer—by a curious sudden mental trick, the girl in gray became a queen in a realm of luxury totally foreign to his surroundings, and strangely beyond reach. That detail annoyed him. He was tired, he knew, and not unnaturally the fresh breath of new surroundings would temporarily unmesh the cogs of memory. He tried to picture Valentine beside him there, and for some reason failed, which disturbed him vaguely, until he explained to himself that of course she was far too fine for such rough environment—no, not quite that—rather say lack of environment. At all events, it would be grossly unfair to drag such a girl as Valentine down—he thought the word "down" very specifically—to such as this. Clearly he must find success quickly and return a conqueror to claim his reward!

From such pleasant contemplations Kent presently aroused, stretched comprehensively, and laughed aloud; the infernal cheek of supposing himself a conqueror tickled his healthy sense of humor. And with that modest conclusion his thoughts returned across the continent from his own gray girl, and, by way of contrast, focused upon the driver's daughter. The blue boyish eyes alone rescued her—he decided in his idle inventory—from the dead level of prosaic plainness.

The embers of the day were sunset red behind the purple mountains when the stage stopped again, some six miles from Farewell Ford, and the girl alighted. Kent was out, too, seeking explanation.

"Why, what's all this? Not deserting the ship, surely?"

She nodded acquiescence and a reason all at once. Following the direction indicated, he spied a cabin set at the edge of a plowed field, a hundred yards or so from the road.

"There's no place just like it!" She laughed bravely, catching up the thread of their last conversation. "At least, there'll be none better when the alfalfa blooms."

It seemed altogether wrong to leave her there, alone. As for the shack, Kent made out a door and a double window in the unpainted front—then, across a furrowed field, there appeared another house, with an outbuilding or two and a friendly wreath of smoke showing bluely against the shell-pink evening sky.

"At least you have neighbors," he said for the sake of saying something reasonably cheerful.

"Oh, yes, indeed. They keep my pony over there. It's really very pleasant." She spoke defensively. "And isn't my mountain beautiful? He's down on the map as The Chief, but I call him Brother Bill . . . it sounds more homey and we're really great friends."

"Well, don't get lonely," admonished Trumble, preparing to move on. Kent climbed up beside him.

"No indeed, Dad. Why, the old Pilot there is the best company in the world." The long shadow of the butte lay across her little ranch. "Good-night."

The horses plodded on as she turned into the field before her shack.

"Got 'er chew?"

Kent admitted being chewless, adding that he didn't happen to use tobacco.

"An' don't eat grass neither, I s'pose?"

"No." Kent was innocent of the time-honored jest.

"So then yer ain't fit company for man or beast," Trumble concluded sourly, and immediately, to show he didn't in the least mean it, began pleasant inquiries concerning Bishop Rudd, to whom he always referred as the "Bish," and as often as not with profane embellishments of his own peculiar blend.

"By the way, the Bishop gave me letters to a couple of men at Farewell—I've got the names here somewhere." The passenger fished a notebook from some pocket, found the page, and deciphered the memorandum by the afterglow. "Do you know a Mr. Jones and a Mr. Colton?"

"Know Fair Jones 'swell's know my pipe—he runs th' paper at Farewell. But tother one—Mister Colton, you say? Blasted if I knew there was a he of that brand loose, an' I cum blame near knowin' every bygod critter in the county."

Kent looked again.

"Yes, it's Colton, all right."

Trumble appeared puzzled.

"Maybe that gal's been deceivin' me," he growled in the direction of the off wheeler.

"That's funny. Why, the Bishop said Colton was one of his best friends. In fact, now I remember he used the words 'my most useful helper.'" The young man ruminated over the mystery. "Anyway," he added, "whomever it belongs to, it's a bully name—Crete Colton. I don't think I ever——"

"*Crete* Colton?" Trumble's explosion cut him short. After a full minute of apoplectic guffawing, the young man, more mystified than ever, demanded explanation.

"Why, *Crete* Colton"—the name acted on the little driver like a pinch of snuff, and his mirth burst forth anew—"*she* ain't no man—no more'n I'm a girl"—good-natured guffaws—"she's a woman."

Kent felt crestfallen. On consideration, he perceived that "Crete" did have a feminine sound, after all.

"So you're introjuiced to Miss Crete, be yer—an' by th' Bishop?" Trumble considered the matter gravely. "Then I reckon yer all right."

"Thanks. But who is Miss Colton and where will I find her?"

For some unaccountable reason the inquiry projected his companion into another spasm of laughter, this one resented by Kent, who was tiring of his humorous blunders.

"What's the joke now?" he asked testily.

"Oh, of course I hadn't ought ter laugh like this." The old man dried his eyes. "But yer see, we've left *Mister* Colton on the road back——"

"Passed him—that is, her?"

"Yes'n no. Not passed her—jist left her. Yer see, Crete Colton's sat here on th' seat with me clear in from Shaniko!"

Kent was speechless. The dusty haired traveler—the hungry girl of Biggs—Crete Colton!

CHAPTER V

KENT GETS A JOB

FAREWELL started life with a firm resolve to attain greatness. While fulfillment of this righteous ambition came slowly, ample preparation, at least, had been made for its attainment in the ambitious generosity with which the town had been "laid out."

At the time of David Kent's advent, Farewell's empty avenues were girded principally by rows of white lot stakes marching toward the four points of the compass in measured procession, the entire civic hollow square of optimism and progress being hemmed round about by persistent sagebrush, junipers, and sand.

The broad expanse of "Main Street" was banked by one- and two-story buildings, with the exception of a solitary structure, whose triple-tiered pretension had earned for its owner the lasting sobriquet of Three Story Olsen. Nearly all the buildings were contemporaneous, for Farewell, born without premeditation, coincident with the timber rush some six years previously, had been weaned with almost indecent haste.

Kent Gets a Job 43

David Kent strolled along one of Main Street's wooden sidewalks. The mid-morning sun was pleasantly warm, and the shadows pleasantly cool. A mob of chattering juniper jays rioted among the needles of a pine whose erect brown trunk was as colorful as burnished copper. Beneath the branches a glimpse of laughing river, timbered slopes, and snow-crowned mountains offered grateful contrast to the dusty street.

In the open door of what purported to be a furniture store, an individual with short red hair and amazingly wide, lilac suspenders sat reading a newspaper. A symmetrical brown arc on the sidewalk, centering at his chair and some five feet distant, witnessed the infallibility of his range. Kent blundered full into the circle's danger zone at precisely the instant when the red-haired reader lowered his paper long enough to sight and fire.

"Gosh, I'm sorry—never seen you." The furniture man, profuse in apology, removed traces of the accident with a hectic bandana.

Kent shouldered the blame, and, having nothing else to do, accepted a proffered chair. An auto-introduction ensued, disclosing the owner of the lilac braces as Jeb Watterson, furniture dealer by vocation and deputy sheriff through political virtue, which is by way of saying he always voted the ticket straight.

"Looking for investments?" The inevitable question came in due course; in a new country everyone has something to sell and every stranger is regarded as a "prospect."

"No, indeed. I'm looking for a job."

Jeb was disappointed, and showed it. "What kind?"

"Oh, any kind." He didn't mean it to sound toplofty, but it did.

"Huh!" a segment of the mahogany-colored arc was reinforced. "Jes' as lief as not handle John D.'s business or be Taft's secretary, I suppose."

The young man, unwithered by the sarcasm, laughed good-naturedly.

"No. They tried to get me but the salary didn't suit. What I want is something speeded pretty modestly. You see, I think I'm going to like it here, so I want to stay, if it's possible to make a living."

Jeb mollified visibly.

"Tried the company—th' irrigation layout? It's two fifty per." Kent shook his head. "Or th' mill?"

"Not yet. But I'll manage not to starve to death, somehow."

"Hope so." The speaker's face expressed no lively concern, however. Then, as Kent moved off, he added calmly: "If you should, jes remember I've got a crackerjack line of coffins—warranted handmade, all sizes and styles, and terms to suit."

The office of the *Pioneer* stood at the end of Main Street. Not actually at the end of the street itself, of course (that was half a mile farther on), but like an architectural rear-guard stationed well beyond the last rank of the sprawling buildings—if not a *finis* to its story of development at least a "to be continued" marking the close of a first chapter. The building was a square box of unpainted boards. A high false front gave the impression of two stories, if regarded head on, but the deception was apparent from any other viewpoint. An ambitious sign announced the name of the paper, and, in letters more modest, that Pharaoh Jones, in addition to being "Prop." was a notary public, while a flyspecked placard in a front window offered these further particulars: "Real Estate, Hunting and Fishing Licenses, Insurance."

Pharaoh Jones was tall, with a large head, and a body thin beyond belief. His most prominent feature was an abnormally bulging forehead, its remote borders fringed with wisps of colorless hair. Below this dome, a face peculiarly small and webbed by scores of tiny wrinkles regarded life with a gentleness all too mild for a country printer, who needs be a steely hearted cynic to survive successfully the pangs and arrows of his calling.

"Mr. Jones?"

"At your service."

"My name is Kent—David Kent. Bishop Rudd told me to look you up; here's a note from him."

Again the young man found the Bishop's friendship an open sesame; the emaciated editor grasped his hand, ushering him to the best there was—the editorial swivel chair.

"Put your weight a mite to the left," the host advised. "It's out of order, that chair—needs doctorin'."

It was apparent to Kent that the chair's owner might well begin his doctoring at home. But of himself Pharaoh Jones said nothing, rambling into ardent recollections of Bishop Rudd, to whom, he stated with winning sincerity, he now owed another debt of gratitude. The younger man returned the compliment, and each found himself liking the other increasingly.

"I want to stay here, at least for a year," Kent finally stated.

Pharaoh Jones nodded approval. With him Farewell was a religion, but one more vitally personal than the usual theological variety is apt to be.

"Couldn't do better," he agreed. "The town has a grand future, and the opportunities for investment are marvelous. With timber, water power, irrigation, wheat lands, and—" but there the swelling list was checked by Kent's smiling interruption.

"Yes, indeed, I've heard a lot about the resources. The only one omitted so far is your own optimism—that's worth at least a thousand horsepower to a community! Why, I'm sure

Kent Gets a Job 47

you and the *Pioneer* could make a city anywhere!" The praise, playful as it was, warmed the sallow cheeks with color.

"It's kind to put it that way."

Kent was building upon a groundwork of white lies, having never seen a copy of the *Pioneer*.

"By the way, may I see your last issue?"

"Certainly." There were a number of pyramids of *Pioneers* beneath a counter facing the entrance, with dust of varying thickness upon them, according to their longevity. From a pile that was scarcely gray, the visitor received one of last Wednesday's papers.

The *Pioneer's* front page was not innocent of advertising; in one corner the Farewell Bank of Commerce blossomed, surrounded by an enticing border of corpulent money bags, and in the other P. A. McPherson addressed an eager public concerning "town and country property." The six modest "heads" lured readers to the details of a school picnic, a rumored railroad, a new homestead law, the satisfactory crop outlook, the county court proceedings, and the development plans of the Bonanza Irrigation Company. The back page was occupied exclusively by an advertisement of the "exceptional opportunities offered settlers on the rich segregation" of that same company. The land, one learned, was free—"absolutely free" was in two-inch blackface type—payment being only for the water right under the munificent provisions of the Carey Act.

On page two was the *Pioneer's* one luxury, an editorial column. To be sure, it was sometimes occupied by boiler plate, when the editor "didn't get 'round" to filling it, but the words "Editorial Column" were always there, a monument to mental travail and journalistic pride.

Below the notice that produce would not be accepted in payment for subscriptions, there appeared the couplet, "Read by all, believed by some, cussed by a few, hated by none." Motley advertisements (among them Jeb Watterson's) divided the honors of pages two and three with boiler plate "news of the world in brief," mostly seven weeks old, and a column or two of "locals" and country correspondence.

Under the caption "Important Debate at Cloverhurst" Kent read far enough to learn the subject of discussion: "Resolved, that money does more harm than drink." His hearty laugh rattled the editorial chair to the verge of collapse.

"Do they often pick subjects like that?" he asked. Pharaoh nodded, gently smiling.

"Well, money isn't likely to injure me irreparably just now—but as I don't happen to drink there's no ground for comparisons!" Kent chuckled.

The mention of money reawakened thoughts which had occupied him earlier on this first day in Farewell. He wanted neither work nor money especially, but the latter he needed, if he were to

Kent Gets a Job 49

follow out fully the conditions of his financially disenfranchised venture.

"Mr. Jones, I'm broke." He delivered himself squarely.

There is not the slightest doubt that Pharaoh Jones had heard similar declarations before. The pained cloud that darkened his sympathetic face intimated perplexity.

"Oh, don't worry!—all I want is advice," the young man added hastily.

"Please don't think of it that way." There was real distress in the editor's tone. "A friend of Bishop Rudd's . . . a friend of mine, sir . . . anything I have is at your . . ."

"Lorsy me! There you go again!"

The interruption came from a motherly woman, built squarely and with a bonny face, who emerged from behind the type cases.

"Pharaoh, what are you giving away now?"

"But, Mother . . ."

"But me no buts!" The command brought the editor up abruptly on the threshold of his explanation—so abruptly that he coughed again.

Kent anticipated a stormy scene, but the expected did not happen. Instead, Pharaoh's better half all at once melted from a domestic dictator into a very womanly helpmate. Her arm was on his thin shoulder when she continued. "Pharaoh, dear, excuse me now. I didn't mean to interrupt, only I got listening and thought someone was borrowing money from you."

4

Pharaoh needed no mollification. At his wife's words the smile returned to the pale, grave face. He introduced Kent.

"You came in the nick of time. Your husband was on the point of giving me the *Pioneer!*" Kent laughingly asserted.

"Th' measles'd be less trouble, and about as profitable. I have to watch him like a baby." Mother Jones harped back to her original theme. "I'm usually back there in the shop setting type, and every time there's a caller I'm in fear and trembling lest he'll get taken in on some scheme. Give him a chance an' he'd have his life insured —or try it—once a week. But book agents is his *bait newer*, as the French say. The dear man'll buy anything if they keep after him hard enough—just like he'll let these patent medicine houses talk him into cutting advertisin' rates in half."

"Now, Mother, please don't," Pharaoh, foreseeing what was coming, pleaded resignedly.

"But that's just what I will, Fair dear. It's right for Mr. Kent to see all your wickedness at the start." The biggest sort of a dimple deepened in one cheek, well above the chubby curve of her double chin. "He *looks* like a decent moral man, doesn't he?"

Kent nodded. Pharaoh assuredly did.

"But he isn't. Oh, don't interrupt!" She smothered signs of protest from the embarrassed editor. "There's no use denying it when the proof is right here." She indicated a bulky box, prodigally nailed, lying beneath a desert of dust in an obscure corner.

"You see, Mister Kent," the mystery wrecker continued, "one day when I was out at the ranch a book agent corralled Pharaoh. He's never explained how it was done, but when I came back he had contracted to buy a set of books on the installment plan, at four dollars a month for ten months. That was last October, and we're still paying, though we haven't enough money to get alfalfa seed."

"And the books? Did they suit?" Kent asked.

"They'd have suited *him* all right, only I saw them first!" Indignation blazed in her motherly face. "What do you suppose those books were?" She put the query breathlessly, answering it herself: "*The complete Writings of Guy du Maupassant!*"

Kent, who was familiar with the racy raconteur, gurgled, heroically suppressing his inclination to laugh aloud.

"And me a member of the church!"

"But, Mother, I've told you, I didn't know," Pharaoh put in.

"It's the first time I've ever doubted his word, Mister Kent." The good woman showed signs of real distress. "Oh, it was cruel hard! He told me they was all about French life, like a history, you know, and as he'd signed for the set and paid something I let 'em come. The first story I read was called *In the Conservatory*. I thought perhaps I'd got a wrong book, so I looked into some of the others . . . and they were worse! As for the pictures, why, land sakes, the clothes in all of 'm wouldn't make covering enough for one decent woman! The whole thing was a living scandal! So I gave Pharaoh his choice—me or the books. And . . . and . . . well, when I showed him the poison he'd bought, he nailed 'em tight in that box . . . it'll never be opened."

"Never," echoed Pharaoh. It might be his tone was faintly tinged with regret.

"We're paying for them yet," she continued. "They're so terrible we don't dare let folks here know we have 'em. The disgrace . . . oh, dear, dear . . . forty dollars' worth of scandal with us so poor! . . . And we can't even give them to the library!"

Mother Jones's description of her spouse's encounter with the book agent was scarcely completed when an automobile drew up in front of the *Pioneer* office.

"It's Mister Failing," Miranda ejaculated uneasily.

Forthwith the floor creaked beneath the weight of a big, square-bodied man, and into the office came the manager of the Bonanza Irrigation Company.

"I'd like to talk with you, Jones," he announced curtly.

Kent Gets a Job 53

Failing's voice was extraordinary. Instead of the deep boom somehow expected from such a bull-like build, the words came forth in a staccato reminiscent of the hero at a Punch and Judy performance. The contrast of the littleness of the voice with the bigness of the man was ludicrous.

Good nature is normally a fat man's prerogative, and whatever his mission the manager contrived to appear no exception to the rule, so far as concerned outward appearances. But behind the smiling mask of his broad pink face lurked hints of things less pleasant. The small, wine-colored eyes were moist and apt to evade direct encounters. The wide brow sloped back quickly. The heavy broadness of the lower face contrasted oddly with the rather skin-drawn appearance of cheekbones, nose, and brow. An inconsiderable amount of unhealthy hair added further to the impression of a structure massively founded but slighted by architect and builder as it rose.

On Failing's hint, Mother Jones and Kent retired to the printshop, whither the manager's queer voice penetrated more than once as he talked with Pharaoh. That shop, Kent observed, offered a notable contrast to the "front office." Absolute spotlessness reigned in the realms of type, for the *Pioneer's* workroom was as amazingly clean as its sanctum was dirty. The rail was the dividing deadline.

"It's Pharaoh's idea," she explained. "He's editor, and I'm only assistant, you see. I'm not supposed to interfere in the office. He says he knows where everything is and if I clean up it bothers him, so he takes care of that side of the rail himself. But in here I just naturally like to keep things neat."

"It's quite remarkable," Kent said truthfully. The floors of printships normally are cluttered outrageously but the *Pioneer* was as clean as a Dutch kitchen. The leads, slugs, and reglets were stored neatly in remodeled cigar boxes, even the type cases were dustless, the Gordon jobber was as resplendent as the nature of job presses permits, and the polish of the windows would shame the untidy instincts of any predatory fly.

In due course Pharaoh joined them.

"Well, I've got 'em. Two months' work, Mother." The editor methodically assorted a sheaf of papers, and impaled them upon the hitherto naked job hook.

"The contracts?" asked Mother Jones.

Pharaoh nodded. "And a lot beside . . . more work than we've seen since the timber rush."

Yet the editor sighed, and his wife showed no elation over this avalanche of prosperity.

"What did he say . . . ?"

Instead of answering, the tired-eyed editor communed with himself for a full minute, until Kent suddenly remembered these were private matters.

"Well, I do hope everything's all right. I must

be going now ... pressing engagement, you know!"

Pharaoh regarded him silently, with speculative eyes, evidently occupied by some disturbing problem.

"If there's anything I can do ..." Kent, about to go, held out his hand.

"Busy?" Pharaoh showed no desire to speed the parting guest.

"Lord, no!"

"Then sit down. I'm not ... well, quite comfortable. I'd like to ... er ... it'd be a real favor to talk things over with you ... you being fresh from the outside, a stranger and all that, could give good advice. And besides, you'll know all about it later."

A synopsis of the editor's narrative, which included most of Farewell's biography, impressed itself upon his listener. James Failing practically supported the *Pioneer*. For two years the Bonanza full-page advertisement had proved a veritable windfall to the little paper, while the irrigation office provided more than half of the job work. To be sure, this latter in the past had chiefly applied on the payment for a forty-acre ranch bought by Pharaoh from the company, but this particular batch of work meant cash. And cash, explained practical Mother Jones, implied means of planting alfalfa and "lots of other things." A crisis had been pending ever since the *Pioneer* voiced criticism of the company ten days ago, and they had momentarily expected Failing's wrath to fall upon them.

"Oh, I hated it, all right." Worry made Pharaoh cough.

"Never mind, Fair dear," his wife comforted him. "We're spoiled, that's all, because we have so little trouble."

"As soon as you were gone Failing opened up in that idiotic voice of his. He didn't threaten much or fly off the handle—if he had, I'd have told him to take his dirty business and be damned!"

"Sh! Why, Pharaoh!" But despite her admonition, one imagined Mother Jones secretly gloried at the rare rebellion.

"Well, I would." He was quite grim—for him. "Of course, he was mad about the settler's letter, and when I wouldn't tell him who wrote it he nearly blew up. The letter, Mr. Kent? Oh, you see we published a letter signed 'A Settler,' which protested because the Irrigation Company was trying to sell more land before it had delivered water to the people who'd already bought."

"Great Scott, *that* isn't allowed, is it?"

"Oh, isn't it? I should say so! It's rotten, but it's being done every day. Take the Federal Southern, for instance." He referred to a well-known irrigation fiasco of a dozen years since. "Land was sold there and money collected. Settlers moved in and started clearing. Then it was discovered there wasn't enough water to care for half the acreage. Of course, the company went bankrupt—after it had been milked dry by the promoters—and the settlers were left on their backs."

"That letter must have been rather fine, then? Who wrote it?"

Pharaoh hesitated.

"Oh, I beg pardon. Of course, that's a secret. But can't the settlers get justice . . . from the State . . . or somebody?"

The editor smiled a bit wearily.

"Apparently not. You see, they choke off all complaints. Mighty little ever becomes public when it's a case of a few busted settlers against a big corporation. Why, even the papers down in th' City won't print anything about settlers' troubles . . . pretend it hurts development and all that."

Next, it appeared, Failing had told the editor that thereafter he did not expect to see any criticism of the company in the *Pioneer*. "If you can't find something good to print, don't print anything," was exactly the way he phrased it.

"Then he went on to say his advertising was nothing but a meal ticket for us, intimating we'd probably starve to death without it. He said the ad. did them no real good and our job prices were away above th' City's—which is true—I know it. Why, even the meal ticket part's correct—charity from such a source—it's just *hell*." The tall wasted man bowed down beneath the unkindness of it all. His shabby suit seemed more ill fitting than ever, his face more pinched, his eyes wearier.

"Yes, I took them. It was that . . . or war." Pharaoh's voice was husky. "And now I suppose we're gagged . . . the poor settlers . . . and sir, what hurts worst is *I know we're right.*"

Mother Jones, with face averted, was suspiciously quiet.

"Shall I send 'em back?"

If the editor's wife had nodded, James Failing would shortly have received an instructive surprise. But in due course she looked around and did not nod. Instead she said, with a brave effort at a smile:

"Fair dear, we'd like to, but we can't . . . just yet. Some day, when the ranch is in crops and the *Pioneer's* a daily, we'll show him! . . . And now we've a very great deal to do, and Wednesday's paper not all in yet."

Saturday was nearly half gone. Mother Jones, fortified with a long gray apron, took a stick of type from the forms on the stone, and once more the soft click-click of the lead letters, scattering into the cases as her skilled hand distributed line after line, made printer's music in the shop.

"You wanted—a—er, that is occupation?" As "job" sounded harsh, the more polite word was substituted.

The young man with seven dollars and thirty-five cents nodded a vigorous affirmative.

"We'll need help." Emerging from his abstraction, the gaunt man delivered himself like an oracle.

And thereafter, with no ceremony at all and a deal of good-natured haggling (each party bargaining *against* himself) a pact was entered into whereby David Kent, volunteer camper on the trail of success, assumed the high office and modest duties of general assistant to the staff of the *Pioneer*.

CHAPTER VI

SUNDAY AT LITTLE EGYPT

On a morning of a Sunday in June, David Kent journeyed toward Little Egypt, as Pharaoh Jones had inexplicably named his ranch adjoining Crete Colton's, some four miles from Farewell. Agamemnon, Pharaoh's mature horse, furnished leisurely motive power for the buggy whose seat the young man shared with the neighbor landlord, or lady, of the Little Egyptians.

It was not until Agamemnon evidenced overwhelming sleepiness on the outskirts of town that Kent abandoned conjecturing the contents of a fat letter from Valentine, which now metaphorically burned in his coat pocket with the pleasurable mystery of all unopened envelopes. Their steed's somnolent tactics, however, returned the young man's wandering attention and his manners. Whipping the horse, he began talking to the girl.

"Aggie isn't a very successful sleep walker," he observed. "And, speaking of sleep, I suppose you're pretty tired yourself?"

She was. Yesterday the school term had ended in that function whimsically called commencement. The responsibilities of directing her charges through recitations, of greeting their parents tactfully, and of looking attractive, and yet not too attractive to be efficient (in the estimation of the School Board) still weighed upon her. Laughingly, she recounted the complex difficulties of eighth grade pedagogy.

"And the worst of it is, I like it," she added.

"There it is again!"

"There is what? I don't understand.'

"Oh, you and the Bishop and Pharaoh are all the same. You like your work." He turned to her in a burst of confidence. "The Bishop gave me a bully sermon along those lines. You see, I never did much of anything back East, and I didn't like what I did. Everything was a beastly bore. Then along came Rudd and told me it was all my fault, and through him I came out here."

She nodded. "Do you like it?"

"Tremendously. That's the funny part. I haven't found much to do yet, except potter around the paper, but that suits me down to the ground . . . if there was only more of it." The sunshine seemed to have filtered into the young man's heart. His words were buoyant, like his eyes. "You see, Miss Colton, I simply *must* make good."

"Everyone feels that way . . . on June mornings," she laughed. "But who put the novel idea in your head?"

"Rudd."

"And what will the Bishop do if you disappoint him?"

"It isn't him I mind. It's—" But there sudden embarrassment halted Kent.

"Oh!" said Crete Colton.

"Engaged. I thought so," was the girl's mental comment.

"After all, I'm not engaged. Wish I were," was the man's thought.

Each of them was quite impersonal, so far as consideration of the other was concerned. To the girl, the man wore the badge of another woman and therefore was satisfactorily safe. As Kent believed, he was Valentine's, and Valentine—he hoped—was to be his, and so the field of feminine attraction was filled. Nurtured in this neutral security their acquaintanceship had ripened pleasantly.

The gray-tinted juniper trees hung heavy with clusters of berries, old blue and opal in color, and about their branches frolicked juniper jays, the blues of their backs and wings harmonizing with the tones of their namesake trees. A pair of newly wedded nuthatches alternately preened their feathers and bathed in the brown dust. The straight columns of pine trees here and there contrasted with the gnarled junipers, lifting needled greenery against the morning sky. The scent of sage was poignant and countless thousands of tiny white starflowers twinkled in the sand, out-smiling the bright sun itself, and defying its parching rays.

Sunday at Little Egypt 63

Agamemnon proceeded to the center of the flat lying between Farewell and the Pilot and there halted without apparent cause.

"Force of habit," was Miss Colton's answer to Kent's look of inquiry. "Did you notice how Jeff Bayley's horse always stops in front of Anderson's saloon?"

Kent had; an historic story related that when Jeff's horse was stolen it subsequently deserted the thief and one morning two weeks later appeared of its own volition at the accustomed post before Anderson's, bringing back to Jeff an excellent saddle he had never before seen.

"Yes. But what has that got to do with it?"

"It's habit with Aggie, too. These lots belong to Pharaoh, and he always stops here to build castles in the air . . . that is, cities in the dust."

"Good Lord! So Pharaoh owns these! Why, we're a mile and a half from town. I hope they didn't cost him much."

"Oh, I consider them very good property." The girl was on the defensive at once. "You know, when the town has 25,000 people, or even 10,000, these will be worth a lot of money."

"*When.*" He emphasized the adverb. "Why not *if?*"

She shook her head in mock despair.

"Don't be a pessimist. It's against the law in Oregon! Some day you'll have to eat your words. Besides they didn't cost Pharaoh much of anything, as he took them for advertising." Then she added gravely. "I do hope he will be able to sell. Poor people, they need money so badly."

"And how about ranchers without water for crops—young lady ranchers, for instance?"

The pointed inquiry brought a flush to her face.

"That's different. I'm—er—ranchers are strong and if they are young, there's plenty of chance later to make up for lost time. . . . Go along, Agamemnon."

Thereafter Agamemnon concentrated on his task, and conversation languished.

Upon their arrival at Pharaoh's they found him seated upon the doorstep, where the sun warmed his gaunt frame and the Pilot and the mountains behind it offered a cheerful outlook. His attention, however, was focused upon a paper, while his forlorn expression seemed in keeping with the poverty-stricken appearance of the paintless shack at his back.

Greetings exchanged and Agamemnon disposed of, the two men set to talking while Crete "ran over" to her own shack a quarter of a mile along the lateral ditch. On the morrow she moved out from town for the summer ranching, and she must "see about things," an indefinite and everlasting feminine prerogative in household affairs.

"A bonny lass," said Pharaoh.

"Very attractive," Kent assented, thinking more of his letter, still unread, than of his words.

"She should be married." Good Mother Jones, emerging from the house, voiced the universal verdict of the court of womankind, that tribunal without appeal. Like wives the world over her instincts were a matchmaker's. Whether the motive be charity or spite, the commandment seems to be: "Do unto others as has been done unto you."

"Are there—prospects?" Kent put the question discreetly.

"There are and there aren't," Mother Jones compromised, with a trace of embarrassment.

"Worse luck!" Whoever, or whatever, was at the bottom of it evidently riled the editor. He sputtered: "The thing I can't understand is what a girl like her sees in a man so doggon hateful as F——"

"Sh-h! For shame, Fair!" Miranda's hand, capably applied to his mouth, stifled her spouse's outbreak.

"Women," said Pharaoh, seizing the luxury of the last word when his wife had departed, "are beyond all understanding."

Kent subscribed to the sentiment with a charitable smile and betook himself to the shade of a juniper tree and his letter.

The epistle contained four pages of routine news (through which Kent hurried), two pages of self-doubting (read with restive frowns), a page and a half of lover-like loneliness (reread thrice, with tender delight), and half a page of announcement extraordinary.

The first section was humdrum, concerning such

items of everyday metropolitan life as new frocks, matinées, and a contemplated visit from Cousin Cecile who lives in Baltimore. The second, whose penmanship hinted distress, hinged upon the difficulties of constancy to the lover far away, indicating a belief that after all perhaps absence does not make the heart grow fonder. Also, it appeared that for once Mamma and Dads were entirely agreed, their meeting ground the mutual belief that she, Valentine, would do well to forget her sentimental bargain with young Mr. Kent. "Aren't they too horrid for words, David dear?" this portion of the letter concluded. To which David added a fervid "Amen," and one or two other things. The loneliness and David-want portion of the letter requires no comment; millions of men and women in the ante-betrothed, post-betrothed, and early married stages have written similarly.

"You may remember that Dads is interested in an irrigation company," the announcement extraordinary proceeded. "An irritation company, I call it, for that is all he seems to get from it. Somehow there's a horrid muddle and poor Dads, instead of making a lot of money, may lose some. He is quite angry and of course it's a dreadful shame that after all he has done they'd treat him so. And David, the wonderful news is that Dads says he must go out and see about it. I haven't told him yet, but *I'm going with him!* Don't laugh—I'll just make him take me."

"Lovingly" was scratched out not so thoroughly as to be indecipherable, and the letter ended "Affectionately, Valentine." Then: "P.S. I'm not sure, but I think the irritated company is in California. That is next door to Oregon so you can come and see me. Are you keeping the rules? I am. V." In very small letters on a margin was this malicious afterthought: "Max Welton will go too."

"Damn," said Kent, at the post-postscript. The rest of it set his heart to beating dance time, and back to the house he went, treading the thin air of daydream paradise.

"What's the trouble, Chief?" Kent had adopted that name for Pharaoh.

"Water rent," was the laconic reply. "Two years of it."

"Oh, you didn't pay last season, then?"

"No. And Crete's in the same boat." Pharaoh whistled *Loch Lomond* through his teeth, contemplating further confidences.

"Well, Mr. Kent,"—he had not yet reached plain "David,"—"you're learning much of our affairs, so you may as well know more. In a nutshell, we're not paying for what we haven't had."

"They've not delivered the water, then?"

"Exactly. Our contract calls for one and eight tenths second feet an acre, and their own measurements of the water in the canal show there isn't enough to supply the sold lands, let alone what they expect to sell. Of course, the water is to be had from the river, and it's simply a matter of enlarging the canal so it can handle greater flow."

"Surely you had some water?" he asked.

"Some, yes. But not enough . . . too little for the crops and certainly a lot less than my contract calls for. As for her," he nodded towards Crete Colton's home, "she was just naturally busted last August. During the early summer, when there wasn't a big demand, they turned a fair amount of water down this ditch so she went ahead and sowed about twenty acres of clover and alfalfa. Then just when the stuff was getting in good shape, and needed water the most, there wasn't any more. So the entire crop burned up."

"She complained?" Kent thought of nothing better to say.

"Complained? God! If it had been me, I'd have used a shotgun." Pharaoh regarded the blue sky gloomily. "Complain?" he repeated. "Say, what's the use of kicking to the Lord when the weather's bad? None, eh? Well, it's just about the same with Failing—'the settlers be damned,' says he, and boosts his salary as manager another hundred."

"It gets you, Mr. Kent." In the pale eyes there burned a something deep of rebellion and sadness, like a child struggling hopelessly against bullying. "Disaster and injustice at close range aren't pleasant. Take Crete. There was about five hundred dollars coming to her from that clover . . . the saving of a year. And it dried

Sunday at Little Egypt 69

and dried and burned brown and went to nothing before your eyes. And what do you suppose she said? 'Better luck next year.' . . . Can you beat *that?*"

Kent pondered the problem.

"Failing admits there's not enough water?" he asked presently.

"Practically. He promises improvements in the system, though."

"I thought you said there was no more money?"

"There isn't, except the maintenance charges, which go chiefly for salaries and upkeep. Of course, we don't know, but it's fairly sure no more capital will invest with things as they are. It's all been going out and nothing coming in. Sales are at a standstill; in fact, there's little land left to sell. The only hope is the South Canal unit."

This solution, Kent knew, contemplated the reclamation of another body of land adjoining the present segregation. The scheme, while skillfully sugared over with plausible advantages, in its naked simplicity was nothing more than a desperate stopgap to redeem the failing fortunes of the Bonanza Company. The new lands were to be watered and sold—or, perhaps, as in the past, first sold and then watered provided the funds held out—and with this fresh revenue the needs of the original segregation could be cared for, scandal turned into success, and (more important in the eyes of the eastern bondholders) interest payments met and sinking funds fattened.

The three-year contract with the State under which the B. I. C. controlled the South Canal segregation would lapse that September, unless an extension of time was granted. Technically, as the company had done absolutely no reclamation, the contract should be annulled at the time limit. But technicalities in the past had received small consideration and it was well understood that an extension could be expected. In view of the heavy investments and losses of the company Failing sought permission to place a higher lien, probably fifty-five dollars an acre, on the new segregation, and as the actual reclamation cost was extremely low, enormous profits seemed assured. Extension of the South Canal contract with the State was therefore the immediate goal of Failing's endeavors.

But in the meantime the Bonanza Company was in perilously deep water, and not a few settlers had sunk for the third time. A vigorous push might bring the tottering structure about the ears of its dictator manager. Whether or not the settlers then would fare worse than ever was an unsolved riddle. As it was, with their annual maintenance fees they virtually were supporting the Failing machine.

"We've decided not to pay our water rent."

"If everyone does it, that will wreck them."

"I reckon." Pharaoh's eyes glinted. "Us or them. Perhaps both. And this summer we'll get enough water if we have to—." His serious glance focused in the direction of the head-gate.

"We'll get it, Pharaoh." Crete Colton, unnoticed by the two men conversing on the doorstep, had returned. "Mr. Failing told me so."

The walk across the plain had heightened the girl's color. Kent resented his suspicion that the manager's name added even a rosier tint. That name, coming when and whence it did, struck her hearers with odd discomfiture.

"Damn Failing," growled the editor, as Crete went indoors.

"Amen," said the young man from the East.

CHAPTER VII

HONEYMOONS, PERFECT AND OTHERWISE

The setting of that Sunday dinner was simplicity itself—a healthy American simplicity.

White curtains and radiantly red geraniums adorned the windows of the shack. Gray building paper neatly covered the walls and ceiling, its chaste expanse unsullied by the usual jaundiced calendars and picture postals. One of Stevenson's gems of optimism had an entire wall to itself, framed with a narrow strip of gray and in its spirit encompassing an eternity of courage. A Reuterdahl sea sketch, in large lines and vivid colors, contrasted with a gracious print of the world-known "Portrait of the Artist's Mother."

"I never saw the ocean," Miranda Jones sighed. "I know I would love it."

"Your mountains are better."

Crete Colton laughed.

"As a rule a man's a fool; when it's hot he wants it cool. And when it's cool he wants it hot, always wanting what is not," she quoted, mocking his gallantry.

Kent took up cudgels.

"Well, Miss Colton, which do *you* want?"

"Both!"

"Dear me, that's a large order. Why so grasping?"

The girl became serious—approximately so, that is.

"Because I've never had either. The nearest I've come to the salt water was on a book voyage to Treasure Island and another with Captains Courageous. The mountains I've *seen*, at least."

Instinctively the four of them regarded those mountains, their crests crisply white just then, with undisciplined cloud halos poising overhead, and below pine-clad foothills, billowing upward to the snowy skyline.

"As for me, I'll never get there. Horses aren't made stout enough," said Mother Jones, good-humoredly, and went to fetch another plate of hot biscuits.

"Nor me." Pharaoh coughed depreciatingly, with the wistfulness that stalks the smiles of the bravest of the sick.

Crete Colton sighed profoundly.

"It's a man's world," said she, wagging a sun-browned finger of scorn at the two males. "Defenseless maidens can do nothing alone——"

"Except work," qualified Mother Jones, returning with the biscuits.

"Of course. I was going to say teach school or ranch. But wait! The time is coming when woman's vote will split man's world in two—like *that!*" Dramatically she divided a steaming biscuit, buttered one half, and ate it.

"Was it the man's half you left?" queried Kent, laughing.

"It was"—buttered biscuit delayed the girl's diction—"*not.* Women prefer men . . . poor things! Beside, as I was saying, we can't do a thing alone—we're actually driven into masculine arms."

Just then Kent could conceive of no better occupation for arms of man than—but what folly of a June moment! . . . There was Valentine . . . Could one imagine *her* in such a madcap mood? Indeed, could butter or hot biscuit be considered in the same mental breath as Central Park West? No. . . . Dignity, elegance, womanly reserve, daintiness . . . At that point, however, catching the eye of the merry militant, he laughed aloud.

"And anyway, Mister Kent," she continued with a twinkle in her blue eyes, "I understand you insisted on making a man of me. . . ."

"Heaven forbid! That would spoil——"

"A perfectly good schoolmarm!" she cut in.

"I was going to say something much nicer," he insisted.

"Then I'm sorry I interrupted. But you will admit you thought I was a man, won't you?"

Kent pleaded guilty to the charge. Dad Trumble had given too generous publicity to that incident of his arrival at Farewell, when he had thought Crete a man's name, to permit denial.

"Well, you're forgiven . . . even if you do think there are nicer things than schoolmarms. And as you really seem contrite I'll admit the mistake has been made before . . . I suppose 'Crete' really is a rather queer name."

"It's original, anyway. How did you fall heir to it?"

"A sort of process of elimination . . . say survival of the fittest," she explained. "You see, my mother's name was Lucretia. When I happened along she set her heart on naming me Lucretia too. But dad objected . . . he said it was altogether too fancy and highfalutin' . . . too much of it for one snub-nosed baby. . . . Dad was a good deal of a Puritan, anyway, and always balked against putting on dog. He wanted to call me plain Mary. Well, of course, I don't exactly remember all the details, but the incident is historically accurate, as the encyclopedia says. Finally they compromised and called me Crete. . . . That pleased mother, because she got most of what she wanted, and satisfied dad, as it seemed neat and simple. So Crete I've always been, and, so far as I know, the only one in captivity."

"Anyway, it gives me a first-class alibi. Also"—there was a wicked glint in David Kent's eye—"it reminds me of another extraordinary name I once heard near Newport News. There was a little darky down there called Fertilizer."

The expectant silence was an invitation to proceed.

"Queer name, wasn't it? Couldn't understand it, so I hunted up the kid's mother and asked her how she happened to give her child such an outrageous name. 'Lawsy, that's a mos' lovely name,' she told me. 'It's jus' as simple an' reasonable as can be. You see, Honey, my husband's name is Ferdinand and my name's Elizah, so we jus' combined 'em when that there first baby come along and called it Ferdilizah.' I agreed with her that it was a lovely name . . . and unique. But to this day I don't know the child's sex."

When the laughter had subsided Kent essayed a return to the former topic of conversation.

"But to get back to the mountains . . ."

"The very thing I most want to do . . . get to those mountains," interrupted Crete. "If I weren't a poor miserable woman," the young man smiled to the point of laughter, and received a grimace for his pains, "a miserable woman, I say —don't interrupt—I'd put a pack on my back and tramp up into those hills. Some day you'd see me waving to you from the top of the Chief. Oh, I could do it, all right—*and I'd love it*." A wistful smile crinkled the corners of her mouth. "Probably the only way I'll ever get such a trip is by marrying someone so there'll be a guide and protector for little me." She was silent for a minute, considering the possibilities of the bargain.

Then suddenly she rushed on, impelled by some secret daydream vision. "Remember how *The Virginian* ends? . . . the wedding . . . no fuss or folderol . . . and then away they went into the hills on horseback, out into the open with just each other and the trees and the stars—that was perfect." She stopped there, and the light shifted from her eyes to her cheeks, where it burned prettily.

"That," said Kent, "would be a perfect honeymoon."

Just then, perhaps fortunately, interruption came in the shape of James Failing's automobile.

Miss Colton was ready for the drive? Miss Colton was not but would be in two minutes. Moreover, this she actually contrived, and in little or no time the car had left the dust of Little Egypt behind it, and three faces in which disapproval was written largely.

As Kent composed page after page of a letter to Valentine, his mind wandered now and again from the task at hand, each time his eyes straying from the letter, and the pocket picture of the proud-faced girl beside it, to the mountains in the West.

"A perfect honeymoon." He repeated the phrase musingly. Scent of pines, music of running water, the stir of the trees, the tang of snowfields, the fragrance of mountain meadows . . . all, in pleasurable imagining, surged through his mind.

"Poor girl," he said, but the compassion sounded hollow, weakened somehow by a suspicion that hers was an affluent poverty.

His eyes caressed the portrayed girl in the dainty frame before him—a face of fine features, calmly aristocratic; deep-eyed, dark-haired, to him the most beautiful face in the world.

So he wrote many pages descriptive of that mountain journey he planned for Valentine and himself, entitling it a perfect honeymoon, and enlarging its details fondly. With a twinge of regretful uncertainty he wound up: "What is *your* idea of a perfect honeymoon?" . . . Twelve days later came the reply: "Rough camping at such a time—ugh! . . . David, in the first place, remember that we are not regularly" (he smiled at the word) "engaged. Of course, you were joking . . . if there's one time in a girl's life when she wants to wear her nicest things, and look her prettiest, and be proudest, it's then. A 'perfect honeymoon,' dear, with only stars and trees for company . . . goodness me, that doesn't sound a bit entertaining."

CHAPTER VIII

THE HORSE CAVE

PRESSING Agamemnon into service as a riding horse Kent started for town toward evening, with the letter just written to Valentine in his pocket.

The west, faced by the rider, was already warm with the preliminary glow of the sunset, like some potter's oven slowly firing.

"The Embers of the day are red, beyond the murky hill,
The bed in the darkling house is spread;
The great sky darkens overhead and the great woods are shrill.
Thus far have I been led, Lord, by Thy will—
Thus far have I' followed, Lord, and wondered still."

"That," said Kent, regarding those dying embers before him, "is perfect."

He repeated the stanza. Agamemnon ambled on, his thoughts occupied, if at all, with his supper. His rider having found in Crete Colton a fellow disciple of the gentle genius of the South Seas, felt grateful to the girl, as though they two had hit upon a dear mutual friend, and as he pursued his way fragments of Stevensonia ran through his mind.

> "The friendly cow, all red and white,
>   I love with all my heart;
> She gives me cream with all her might
>   To eat with apple-tart."

There he was obliged to laugh immoderately at the effect of his declamation upon a jackrabbit, who stood petrified at the roadside, with long ears astonishingly erect.

Having laughed at the rabbit, he laughed at himself, and forthwith became reasonably serious. In which mood the magnet of Valentine again captured his thoughts, and mingling with hair-brained plans for hill-land honeymoons there evolved the question, "Does Val know Stevenson?" Probably, he decided, she did not, for reading was "out of her line." Anyway, Val knew so many other things. The last reflection was distinctly satisfying.

The road to Farewell wound interminably, following the whims of an old cattle trail from which it had developed. So, to save distance and, like the bear who went over the mountain, to "see what he could see," Kent struck off 'cross country in the direction of the town, Agamemnon stalking stiffly through the sagebrush and here and there making detours around outcroppings of lava rock.

And in the lea of one of these, they suddenly

came upon an unoccupied automobile. It was Failing's car, halted where a depression gave entrance to an underground cave.

All at once Kent found himself distinctly ill at ease. The last thing he wanted was to be found seemingly playing the part of shadow to these two.

"Hard a starboard!" Kent tattooed with his heels iron-sided Agamemnon. "We'll get out of this."

Horse and rider swung to the right. As they executed the flank retreat, he recalled hearing of the Horse Cave, chanced upon some years previously when a band of horses coming from the range had disappeared miraculously; the buccaroo finally found them in this cavern, which could shelter two hundred head.

Scarcely was Agamemnon under way when Kent found himself upon the edge of a great hole, perhaps forty feet across, and well hidden by a fringe of sagebrush. Traversing the roof of the cave, they had blundered upon this circular "skylight" where the rocky ceiling had fallen in of its own weight.

Kent dismounted to investigate. And as he stood on the edge of the open cup, suddenly the sound of voices filtered up from among the shadows.

"My idea of a honeymoon" . . . That much Kent heard distinctly; what followed was blurred. The voice was Failing's.

In spite of himself the involuntary eavesdropper almost laughed aloud. It seemed as if he had heard, and thought, and written nothing but "honeymoon" all day! But it was annoying to find Failing setting himself up as a connoisseur in such matters.

"That's disappointing." It was Crete Colton's low-pitched voice.

"Why?"

"Oh, you see, I've made other arrangements." Then followed a peal of jolly laughter, drowning whatever Failing said.

"Someone else? No, indeed! I simply referred to the kind of honeymoon. . . . Tastes differ, you see."

Then he said something about her seeking the man to fill the place . . . just what Kent could not catch, for Failing's peculiar voice had slight carrying power. But whatever the words they roused her.

"I seek no man, Mr. Failing!" she said angrily, stepping out into the open.

Kent was struck by the sudden sternness of the girl. Evidently so also was her companion, for apology gushed forth quickly.

Visibly the girl melted, half hypnotized, it seemed to Kent, by the driving insistency of the man. To see her apparently so pliable left him alternately hot with resentment and clammy cold with apprehension. . . . Stealthily he edged away from the opening, ashamed of having seen and overheard—ashamed, and sorry for Crete Colton.

The Horse Cave 83

The two in the cave acted out their little scene, unconscious of the audience they had lost.

"Won't you call me Jim?" Failing was very close to her, but well in leash.

The blue eyes faltered before the insistent sherry-colored ones—dull, as rich old sherry should be, but just then with a glint of fire in their sophisticated depths.

"Well . . . Jim?"

Failing launched into words then . . . impatient, eager words, telling his love and need for her, with a passionate undercurrent of brutality none too deeply hidden beneath the veneer of his self-control.

Then for long seconds they stood silent, face to face, eye to eye, each taking the measure of the other. The girl saw the male strength, the power, even the latent deviltry of the man; he was bluffly handsome when on his mettle, despite his overlargeness. The man drank in the attractions of the feminine figure before him, the soft hair, the level eyes, the self-possession of the strong inviting mouth; and because she was not a girl to trifle with he craved her the more. . . .

"No," said she.

"Why?" He put the query bluntly.

"Because I don't care to."

He kept his smile.

"Why?"

The doggedness of the tone, of his look, compelled her.

"Are you sure you want to know?"

He nodded.

"It's the things you do."

"You mean—?" The sherry-colored eyes narrowed.

"The irrigation troubles." Then, all at once, she broke down—lost, at least, her poise. "Jim Failing,"—she was close, almost touching him; her hands were before her, perhaps defensively, perhaps in supplication,—"Jim Failing, I know that there isn't water enough for the South Canal, and you know I know it. What is it to be— more broken-hearted settlers?"

The big manager's ruddy face darkened.

"Who told you?"

"Isn't it true?" That was her only answer.

James Failing was deadly still. Slowly the blood surged into his face—then swiftly, until it purpled.

Crete, her head hanging, saw nothing of the danger signal.

"What about the settlers? Please . . . oh, if you'll only give them a square deal . . ."

"The settlers be damned!" Failing blazed with wrath. Would those scurvy settlers forever be cast in his face?

Then, as suddenly as it came, the hot anger left him, and the big face smoothed out.

Failing's eyes focused full upon the trim figure, drinking in its girlish lines with a long, hungering look. Suddenly he stepped close beside her and

The Horse Cave

boldly, almost triumphantly, he turned the girl's face upward from beneath its protecting crown of pale hair. . . . With his two great hands pressing against her cheeks the manager smiled down into Crete's eyes, seeking in them an answering smile, or, at least, a signal of submission. . . . So he poised tensely over her.

The blue eyes neither smiled nor faltered, but met his steadily, and neither fear nor invitation was written in their depths.

For an instant they stood thus, and then the muscles of James Failing's body all at once relaxed, the smile faded from his face, and his hands fell to his side.

"I beg your pardon. . . . Please . . . forget."

The quiet acceptance, the sudden extinction of his inner fire, came most unexpectedly of all. And as Crete Colton silently followed the manager to the car, she felt queerly grateful.

CHAPTER IX

"UNTIL THE RESURRECTION"

"HARD TIMES" was the password as summer ripened. While the rainbow of the future beckoned as brightly as ever, the pot of gold at its foot seemed securely beyond the reach of even Farewell's indomitable optimists. Irrigation development was at a standstill, railroad rumors were few and far between, and even the usual bickerings of an isolated community lagged as the dusts deepened.

As Kent's apprenticeship wore on he became more and more an integral part of the *Pioneer's* little family and increasingly familiar with the duties of his adopted calling. Nor did the familiarity breed contempt. He even learned to respect the superlative importance of "locals," those golden nuggets of country journalism. Dog fights, country shoppers, and all the multitudinous incidents of everyday life became grist for his pencil, ultimately appearing as "Bits About Town," interspersed with "reader ads." declaiming the universal virtues of Somebody's Bitters or the fact that Mrs. Olsen desired to sell a calf of approved ancestry and winning personality.

"Until the Resurrection" 87

By degrees the young Easterner came to know the people of Farewell and through them the irrigation story unfolded. Gathering its various threads, sifting and piecing fragments together, Kent gradually constructed in his mind a clear outline of the situation. Then one night in his tent (a happy-thought summering shelter close to the river) he put his findings in words, setting down the history of the project in unvarnished detail.

On the following morning the young man placed the fruit of his labor on the editor's desk together with some tidbits of minor town news.

It was a Tuesday, and Wednesday was publication day for the *Pioneer*. In the shop the soft clicking of type as Mother Jones marshaled them into the stick was more rapidly determined than upon an easy-going Saturday when the left-overs from the preceding issue were set up.

Pharaoh sat in the erratic swivel chair correcting galley proofs and in the due course of his labors his attention fell upon Kent's offering. The "locals" he slapped on the copy hook with a grunt of approval and turned his attention to the irrigation article.

Pharaoh read, then, the story of the Bonanza Irrigation Company which he already knew so well; how the reclamation started with a blare of trumpets and golden promise; how the first water was taken from Welcome River and distributed out upon the thirsty soil through canals and ditches; how sales commenced and thousands of acres were deeded to settlers before either ditches or water were within miles of the land; how unforeseen obstacles and expenses were encountered, the costs far exceeding the estimates; and how finally, the funds had all but run out and still there were scores of settlers who had purchased, or made partial payment upon, tracts and received contracts for water service, and who now could not get that very water for which they had contracted and upon which their entire fortunes depended. Then, as Kent outlined, had come charges that there was not enough water available in Welcome River to supply the lands which the State had authorized for sale, even if the necessary ditches could be built. But this accusation was speedily exploded when an official investigation and measurement of the water flow disclosed the fact that not only was there sufficient water for the original segregation but for the South Canal segregation as well. This latter contained 80,000 acres and the company proposed to reclaim it forthwith.

There was a glitter in Pharaoh's eye as he turned to the last page, and a martial fervor, strangely foreign to it, warmed his gentle face.

"Good Lord!" said Kent to himself, "I wonder if he'd dare publish it?" And thinking of Failing, he grinned.

Pharaoh read on: "The company cannot fulfil its contracts with settlers who have bought land.

"Until the Resurrection" 89

Many of them have not received water and the State cannot, or will not, compel its delivery. The company now proposes to secure more lands from the State, saying that the cash returns from the new project will enable it to complete the delivery system of the first unit. That may be true. Perhaps the cash from sales on the new unit will be used to save the settlers on the present segregation. But if that is permitted, what of those new purchasers? Will they in turn be cast adrift and ultimately left with contracts which cannot be fulfilled and acreage which cannot be watered?

"Emphatically we say this must not happen. And emphatically we declare that if the present plans are followed out, and the company is permitted to develop the South Canal segregation in the way it proposes, those who purchase South Canal land will reap another harvest of tragedy.

"Our duty is clear. We must all strive to prevent the company obtaining the State's permission to exploit the South Canal segregation at the expense of the settler. That development must be permitted only when the interests of the present land owners, and the new land buyers, are absolutely safeguarded.

"Unalterably the *Pioneer* will oppose the South Canal unit plan, as that plan is now presented. We ask that the citizens of Farewell and the settlers of the segregation join with us in this stand."

With the points of his long thin fingers pressed

together, Pharaoh contemplated the pages before him, while their author in turn watched. Composedly one bony hand captured a scrap of copy paper while the other secured the stumpy pencil from above his right ear.

"The Story of Our Disgrace," was the caption he wrote. Below it he penciled this introduction: "For two years the *Pioneer* has been silent, a silence of bondage. The Irrigation Company has held the whip hand and stifled criticism from this or any other quarter. However, here for once are the true facts; the history of the Bonanza Irrigation Company—what it has done and what it seeks to do."

Pharaoh handed his companion the paragraph.

"It's well done," was all he said.

Kent, having read this Declaration of Independence, regarded the tall spare man admiringly, and his admiration was tempered with pity. For the little *Pioneer* to attack Failing seemed sure suicide. If only they were powerful enough to fight the B. I. C. in the open! . . . All at once he thought of his own dollars, idling three thousand miles away; how better could he utilize that renounced income than in such a fight?

"It would take the roof off," said Pharaoh, tapping his lean fingers.

Kent scarcely heard him. He was thinking of the Quixotic rules. He, Valentine, and the Little Bishop had agreed to them . . . he, and his editor friend, must sink or swim as they were.

"Until the Resurrection" 91

"I'm sorry. I guess we can't." There was infinite apology in the simple statement.

"Plenty more chances," Kent replied cheerily.

"Yes . . . the time will come." The editor took from a disorderly drawer a sheaf of papers tied with twine. "We'll keep it with these. You never saw 'em, did you?" Kent shook his head.

"My graveyard," Pharaoh explained, unfastening the string. "Buried alive." He showed some scores of sheets thick with penciled words. "If you don't object, we'll add another corpse—until the resurrection."

The literary cemetery was peopled by defunct articles, most of them two-fisted editorials dealing uncompromisingly with compromising subjects. As the meaning of it dawned upon him, Kent laughed aloud, so infectiously that its proprietor chimed in.

"Excuse me . . . as a chief mourner I suppose it's indecent to laugh, but I can't help it. The graveyard's a fine idea . . . sort of a safety valve."

"Exactly. Most every week something turns up that doesn't suit me. Perhaps it's politics, or county affairs, or local matters; often enough it's this irrigation squabble. So I just turn loose and write a red-hot roast, saying exactly what I think as near the way I'd like to as the Lord'll let me. Somehow it sort of makes me feel better."

"It cools one off," Kent agreed.

Pharaoh nodded. It pleased him mightily not to be misunderstood.

"If I published half of this, there'd be no end of trouble. I want to . . . most of it . . . like everything. But it isn't as if we had money . . . we've got to watch out, Mother and I." He sighed. "And then I'm not exactly strong and if anything should happen . . . well . . . it's best to play safe. And these things,"—his thin hand lay on the discarded writings, and, as he hesitated, his eyes seemed to say, "Please don't laugh,"— "somehow, after I've written 'em and tucked 'em away, it's easy to *pretend* they've been published . . . I actually *feel* as if they had . . . perhaps it's childish, but *this* way . . . why, they don't do any *harm*."

Therein, unwittingly, Pharaoh gave a true measure of his mind and heart.

"Some day we'll run a bunch of 'em in a special edition," said Pharaoh finally, chuckling. "We'll print it in red ink."

"And send a marked asbestos copy to Jim Failing," added Kent.

CHAPTER X

ON HEAVEN AND HELL

PHARAOH JONES received two dollars and seventy-five cents cash for printing five hundred posters one Monday in June. They were on what printers call one-eighth stock, as Pharaoh explained to Leon Callier, who gave the order, offering the observation to cover his astonishment that Failing's man should be interesting himself in a settlers' meeting.

"It would be as reasonable for the condemned to drum up attendance at a lynching bee," he observed to Kent, when the customer had left. "As a rule Failing's chief delight is suppressing settlers' meetings. They and he don't agree for a cent."

"The exception proves the rule, you know," replied the amateur assistant.

"But why in the name of all that's holy should *he* want a meeting of the settlers?" the editor persisted.

"Who said it's a settlers' meeting?"

"This blamed copy . . . as plain as the nose on your face." Pharaoh read aloud the penciled words, heavily underlined: "*Important Meeting of Settlers.* To-night at the Grange Hall."

"Oh, yes, that's plain enough." Kent's skeptical tone showed no conviction. "But *who's* calling the congregation, *why* are they calling it, and when the hat's passed who'll get the collection? That's what *I* want to know."

For a space of several seconds Pharaoh's mild eyes observed Kent. Then they took inventory of the "copy" for the poster, following the scrawled lines from top to bottom with the precision of long-suffering practice. Then all at once the many wrinkles of the small face and its overjutting forehead visibly deepened and crackled, marking the spread of a mirthless smile.

"You think——?"

"I know!"

Kent's ejaculation turned the lines into a genuine smile. Such a positive fellow, this young Easterner!

"Oh, perhaps I'm going too strong on it," Kent added. "But what's the unholy reason behind this sudden interest in settlers' meetings? And why on earth do they spring a meeting on six hours' notice?" As Pharaoh offered no explanation he answered himself. "Because they want to run the works their own way. They're calling it a settlers' meeting so there'll be no comeback. And as you can't get the posters out until the middle of the afternoon, an' the meeting's at eight, of course the chances are slim for much of a crowd

On Heaven and Hell 95

. . . other than the company folks who'll be ordered on deck. Am I right?"

Pharaoh nodded.

"Well, it's not my party, but I intend to take a hand, anyway. While you're printing the bills, I'll drum up attendance for Mr. Failing's privately conducted settlers' meeting . . . without his asking me to take the trouble, and no extra charge for the advertising."

Kent slammed out, and Pharaoh turned to the case.

"The services, I fear, won't be according to schedule," sighed the editor, who scented trouble. And as he slipped the big wooden type into the stick anyone observing his vagrant smile might reasonably have concluded the outlook was not entirely displeasing to the gentle printer.

In the meantime, an automobile floundered on its way from Shaniko, bearing John E. Sanborne, State Water Master, an individual slight of figure, pale of eye, and inclined to baldness and pessimism, the last named state of mind aggravated just then by the recurrent discomforts of the journey.

At the third blow-out of the afternoon the little man who rode with the driver seemed as jovial as ever. His good-natured bantering, as he helped pump up the new tire, annoyed Sanborne.

"You seem to enjoy work." The bald engineer addressed the little optimist testily. His answer was a smile of assent.

"And being delayed, too, I suppose?" persisted Sanborne sourly. "Gives us so much opportunity to enjoy this *grand* country."

"It's a good country." The little man said it with conviction.

"Good as hell!"

"Oh, better!"

The little man laughed, the driver chuckled, and Sanborne felt further aggrieved.

"From an engineering standpoint," he cleared his throat sententiously, "the country is hopeless. It is undermined with faults. Irrigation is a gamble; the water you have to-day may vanish into the ground to-morrow. Ugh! Dust, sage-brush, and juniper! Irrigation is rotten——"

"It is." Sanborne scarcely caught the low-voiced agreement.

"Eh? Yes, it certainly is. Oh, it's hell all right—as an engineer, I ought to know."

"Yes, you ought to. But it isn't hell. You're up on irrigation, but not on hell, sir. As a churchman, such things are my specialty, and this is not hell. In fact—" the little man turned his back on the State Water Master and his face to the western skyline—"to me it's a lot like heaven."

An hour later the car broke down entirely, and the softly swearing driver, the vexed engineer, and the heaven-seeing Bishop set out on foot for Farewell, a matter of six dusty miles.

CHAPTER XI

THE SETTLERS' MEETING

At a quarter to eight James Failing was as uncomfortable as he ever permitted himself to be. In the first place, Sanborne, whom he wanted, had not put in an appearance. Secondly, a great many people whom he did not want were arriving. Judging from the lines of farm wagons and buggies hitched about town, and the knots of men clustering on the edge of the sidewalks, the meeting was to be eminently successful from the standpoint of attendance. Yet its sponsor was anything but pleased. The little snowball he had started was rolling up altogether too unwieldy a bulk.

Tex Darling, the ditch rider, loped down the street, dismounted, and delivered a message to Failing.

"It's all right, boys," the big manager announced to the group about him. "They broke down a few miles east of town, and Dad Trumble's stage'll pick 'em up. You'd better get inside. We'll be starting up soon now."

So the "Company crowd," as they were called, filed up the narrow outside stairs and through the only entrance to the Grange Hall above Jeb Watterson's furniture store. There was sleek Callier, the sales manager, Hartpool, who ran the company's Z X ranch, the office force, and a score of huskies from the camps who got their pay with reasonable regularity and were disposed to do as directed, whether it was a matter of repairing ditches or breaking heads.

The benches filled then with settlers, sunbrowned, unprosperous men with tired, determined faces, and most of them young, as is the way of a new country. There were women, too. One of them brought her latest baby, because there was nothing else to do with it. None of them were old in years, yet none seemed so young as the men, because life in shacks and tents and cooking over sagebrush fires and grubbing with a mattock when there is time for it, and mothering another generation of pioneers, routs Youth prematurely. With the women were Mother Jones and Crete Colton. Pharaoh and Kent, who came in late, found seats near the door.

Shortly the stairs creaked beneath the ponderous steps of the manager, with the State Water Master in his wake, resembling, as Kent thought, a moose breaking trail for a sleek coyote.

Asahel Brush, president of the Water Users' Confederation, occupied the platform with Failing and Sanborne. Brush was an old fellow with a club foot and no love whatever for the company and its methods. But he owed two years' water rent.

The Settlers' Meeting 99

"You preside," said Failing to him.

"Preside yourself," was Brush's gruff reply. "It's your funeral."

"Oh, no, indeed," Failing purred. "This is the settlers' affair . . . you do the honors."

And old Brush did, with extremely bad grace.

Sanborne, after his habit, spoke interminably. He told the old story. The company deserved help, not hindrance; pioneer capital in a virgin field merited protection. But of pioneer settlers he said little. He advised patience. It was perhaps true, he admitted, that the canals just then could not serve all the lands of the original segregation, but this would be cared for in due course. For the present the settlers should be willing to receive less than the amount of water for which their contracts called. So far as he was concerned, there would be little consideration for complaints until the company had been given time to enlarge the ditches.

"When will that be?"

The query came from the back of the room.

"That," replied Sanborne, with a flush showing through his sallowness, "I shall leave for Mr. Failing to explain." And he sat down.

"You have called this meeting——"

"You called it yourself!" As the interruption punctuated Failing's first sentence, there was a stir of sátisfaction among the settlers.

"Who's that?" growled Hartpool beneath his

breath. "The damned anarchists! If I had my way I'd shut 'em out."

"The Ol' Man had a good hunch, anyway," Callier whispered to the ranch foreman. "If so many of 'em hadn't got wind of it we'd have been all right. As it is we'll slip it over anyway." But Hartpool, a man of action, thought the outlook darker than did Callier, the man of plans, and shook his head. For his part he would clean the room and be done with it.

"The meeting was called, anyway,"—Failing corrected himself with a smile that was intended to be conciliating,—"to discuss matters of interest to the settlers. Mr. Sanborne and I have the good of the man on the land closely at heart, and we've worked out a scheme that I am sure will appeal to you all. With your coöperation it can be made a success, and all of us profit."

Failing talked hard and earnestly, and perspired fluently. He admitted the existing canals were not large enough to care for all the lands that had been sold under them.

"It is simply a matter of getting more water from the river and enlarging our canals and ditches." There he paused, as if he had developed a conclusion entirely original.

"Wall," drawled old Asahel Brush, "we're glad you agree with us, Mister Failing. That's exactly what we've been saying for more'n two years. But what are you goin' to do about it?"

"That's just it." Failing smiled benignly upon the chairman.

The big man looked quite triumphant. Although Kent had always distrusted if not actively disliked him, just then, as the manager set forth his case and played his cards boldly, even though realizing that they were not stacked in his favor as he had planned, the young Easterner could not help but admire him.

Failing's scheme was simple. Briefly, he proposed to open up the new South Canal segregation, which could be watered at slight cost, sell the water rights there at a generous figure, and devote some of the profits to putting the original segregation in good shape.

"What we want is your endorsement of the South Canal unit. Our contract with the State covering it expires in September. With your support we can have it renewed, and by next summer we can start the work there and get enough money to enlarge your canals."

The minute Failing sat down Hartpool was on his feet with a resolution in which the settlers went on record endorsing an extension of the contract.

"All in favor of the motion—" someone up in front shouted.

"Ain't no motion put to vote," a hostile voice roared, and half a dozen others added their quota of dissension. Pandemonium was gathering headway, when the door opened and Dad Trumble bounced into the room, with the dust of the road still thick upon him and his horsewhip in his hand. Behind the old driver another figure entered, a small thick man in a black suit and leggings.

The interruption caught the attention of the crowd, momentarily calming the rising uproar.

"Let's hear from Dad Trumble. He knows what's what!"

Good-naturedly the cry was taken up, for the old man was a prime favorite. While they jostled him to the front, the stocky newcomer peered around the room, caught sight of Kent, and tried to edge through the crowd to his side. But he could not reach him, so scrawling a few words on the back of an envelope, he passed it down the line.

"Land Board probably won't grant extension South Canal contract unless settlers O. K. it. Ask Failing why he wants this endorsement. RUDD."

Kent reached the signature with astonishment. The last he had seen of the Bishop was at the Pennoyer dinner in New York, and here suddenly he was turning up with the key to the puzzle! Looking along the crowded bench he caught the little Bishop's eye and signaled his thanks. Then, on an impulse, he was on his feet demanding recognition so vehemently there was no denying him. It was Kent's first gun in the local hostilities, and although the settlers had no idea what he wanted, they knew him as a friend of Pharaoh and indefinitely scented more trouble, which was becoming dear to their hearts.

"Let's hear him!" they howled. And old Asahel announced the floor was his.

"Mr. Failing, why do you want the settlers to go on record for an extension of your South Canal contract?"

Failing, outwardly as cool as blue steel, was on his feet smilingly.

"For the good of the settlers themselves—yes, and the company's too, I admit. The South Canal will save us all. And now may I inquire your interest in the matter?"

The manager's counter question was sharp and cold. But Kent ignored it and came back again.

"If the settlers refuse to endorse this scheme for robbing Peter to pay Paul, can you get the renewal yourself?"

"Mr. Kent,"—the manager's words were biting,—"this is a question of whether the settlers care to help themselves. And as for you, sir, what right have you——"

But hoots of disapproval interrupted him there, and the next anyone knew, old man Trumble had annexed the floor. "Gentlemen," said he, "*and* Mr. Failing,"—an historic witticism which provoked peals of mirth,—"I jes' want ter say a word or two about this here matter. As my frien's explain the doin's ter me, the company wants something from us poor devils of settlers. Now, I ask yer, whenever *we* wanted something, didn't we have to pay for it . . . usually about twice?"

"Yes! Yes!" shouted a dozen, with mixed

anger and laughter, while "Sit down," "Throw him out," and less complimentary phrases gruffly emanated from the front benches.

"An' what are they handin' us? So far as I can see, nothin' at all. We've got contracts for water and the company says it can't fill 'em. For why? Because they're broke, they say. And we all know why they're broke—because"—Failing was on his feet threateningly—"yes, Mr. Failing, I'm talking about you and the other bygod officers!" Little old Dad Trumble blazed up full blast directly in the big manager's face, and there was something about the way he grasped his whip which kept Failing from coming close. The driver was white with anger, Failing white with something that was not entirely anger, and the crowd tensely still.

"It's true, boys . . . true as gospel! This here pirating manager and his gang have sucked the company dry. Oh, we all know it, so why not speak out in meetin'? It's their high salaries and sich that have taken all the cash. *That's* why there ain't enough money to build the ditches to bring us the water we've paid for! An' now they come wanting us to help 'em start another steal."

The old man stopped for a minute, apparently meditating. Yet he was not interrupted. No one would, or could, have broken in on him just then, for his sudden fierce fire carried with it the spirit of the entire meeting.

"Are we sure we're to get any good out of the

new unit? That's what I'd like to know? Suppose they get the contract extended and sell the lands. Will they spend the money in saving us, or will they grab it and leave us holding the sack?"

There Failing contrived to slip in a sentence. About all the crowd heard of it was the words "guarantee bond."

"Another bygod guarantee!" Dad's voice was bitter with scathing contempt. "We've seen contracts, which is guarantees, until we've got the blind staggers studying 'em. The State don't help us get our rights under them, and why should we expect more out of any other kind of bond. Guarantee hell! *What's they worth to a man who'd skunk a girl!*"

The last phrase the old man delivered measuredly, word by word. Every syllable of it penetrated throughout the room. And everyone there knew what he meant; knew that Failing's company, through breaking its contract and not delivering water, had wiped out all of Crete Colton's crop and most of her savings.

The utter silence broke. Tension gave way in suppressed "ahs." Someone swore.

"It's God's truth," said a man in little more than a whisper, and was heard by all.

Then a lank rancher was on his feet.

"Mr. Chairman, let's hear from the lady herself. While we're at it, let's have all the truth."

There was Dad Trumble at the platform's edge, with his threatening whip, and his white wrath.

The sallow engineer wilted in his chair. Failing stood at the side of the platform, red of face and then suddenly white. The look of him fascinated Kent; abruptly the enraged expression turned to fear, and then, curiously, there was neither anger nor dread, but a supplication astonishingly out of place—a subdued, almost feline appeal in the ruddy eyes, softening the hard face until its masculinity seemed somehow to have slipped away. And in wonder Kent turned from the manager to where the manager's suddenly soft eyes were looking.

"Yes, let's hear from her!"

The cry went up for Crete Colton. And because all were looking at her, or toward her, none but Kent caught that expression and that mute message written on Failing's face for Crete Colton's own interpretation.

The girl's mouth opened as if to speak, but she only wet her lips. It seemed as if she were about to rise, but instead she settled all at once more firmly in her seat. And instead of looking to the eager men and women about her, the blue eyes gazed steadily to the stage. . . .

Crete Colton did not speak. Instead—after a space—she smiled and shook her head. And because she was loved more or less personally by nearly every man and woman in the room, she was urged no further.

Disorder returned. For a minute it looked as if the meeting would break up. Then Dad Trumble made himself heard again. This time he had climbed to the platform, and as he spoke the fire seemed gone out of him.

"There ain't no use in a row," he counseled. "I might be wrong. I dunno. Anyway, it's up to all o' us now to get right ca'm agin, and I don't know anyone who can make more headway when it comes to puttin' kerosine on the scrappy waters, so ter speak, than our good frien' Bishop Rudd."

Catching the drift of Dad's remarks heads craned around to locate the Bishop. Everyone at Farewell knew Bishop Rudd, and most of those who knew him liked him.

"So, ladies an' gents, I'm a-goin' to ask the Bish to talk to us, with the permission of the hon'rable chairman."

Bishop Robert Rudd, whose diocese was a railroadless territory vaster than several eastern States, spoke simply and with strong straightforward words which won prompt attention. He said that in disputes both sides usually had a measure of right, and counseled full investigation.

"And as we're here," he continued, "let us take the opportunity to thank the Almighty for what he has done for us, and to pray for his aid and forgiveness . . . I am sure you are all willing."

So the "little Bishop," who had conducted services before the light of sagebrush fires at cattle camps, and in saloons commandeered for the occasion on Sabbath mornings, offered a simple prayer. He asked that strength be given to make more pure the language of those who supplicated, and especially that the taking of the Lord's name lightly should cease. And all joined with him in a resounding "Amen."

It was late. Restless scraping of feet signaled approaching disbandment of the "settlers' meeting." But ere the scraping grew louder the company crowd played their last card, following up the previous lead.

"Mr. Chairman," it was devil-may-care Hartpool speaking. "A while back I put a motion. It was never withdrawn, and I'd like a vote on it."

Silence.

"Question," shouted someone.

Asahel Brush chewed his mustache and finally called the vote.

There was a full-throated chorus of *ayes*.

"Contrary minded."

"*No*," roared the settlers, and the sound of it sent red blood racing to Failing's face, and delight to the heart of Kent.

Asahel scratched his head. Parliamentary procedure and himself were far from intimate. Rudd, leaning over, coached the puzzled presiding officer.

"Them in favor of the resolution rise," said the chairman. The company crowd to a man stood up.

Laboriously old Asahel counted those standing. "Forty-six," said he.

"The noes will stand." The settlers unlimbered their legs.

"Th' baby don't count," said someone, but without getting a laugh.

The chairman stabbed the air in the direction of each voter with his burly forefinger. "Forty, forty-one, forty-two, forty-three—eh, what's that? Forty-four, forty-five—" there he halted—there were no more voters standing.

"Licked, by God!" Dad Trumble's ejaculation rang out in the momentary silence. And then, as the chairman was about to pronounce the result of his count, the little old stage driver again became the central figure of the gathering.

"Lookyhere!" His tone commanded full attention. Before, he had been defiantly passionate; now he was coldly passionless. "Jes' one word, folks afore we go further. It's about this South Canal. What's the use of the new segregation when there ain't water enough for it?"

"What do you mean?" Hartpool barked at him, ready to bound onto the platform.

"Mean? Jest exactly what I say. There ain't enough water in Welcome River to irrigate the new unit, an' *I know what I'm talking about!*"

"Why, you old fool,"—Failing's voice sounded ridiculously small, and his lips were lead colored as he licked them,—"the engineer's measurements show there's plenty of water for both segregations."

"*Whose* measurements, Mister Failing? *Your*

engineer's, eh? An' how much did you pay him to make 'em? An' how much will you give me not to tell what I know? There ain't the water, folks, *an' I can prove it!* Three years ago when——"

"Dad!"

The word came sharp, beseeching from the pale lips of Crete Colton.

Then the company men commenced hooting, while the settlers howled for more information about the water. Suddenly in the midst of the uproar there was a crash near the door—a lamp was down—a flicker of red flame, a scream, and the terror-cry, "*Fire!*"

The thought of the two slits of windows and the door with its narrow wooden stairs struck three men simultaneously. Two of them acted upon the same impulse; with scrambling jumps, executed almost before the slower-witted realized what transpired, Kent and Rudd were beside Crete Colton, and each, in the instantaneous mental record of that moment, realized a swift satisfaction at the other's action. The third man was James Failing. When the lamp fell the manager had been poised on the edge of the platform. On the instant of the warning cry the big man catapulted toward the door, scattering those who blocked his path like a mad bull charging among sheep.

In a moment the uproar was uncontrolled. Few knew what had happened. The one thought was of the door. Swift panic had turned a roomful of sane humans into a den of trapped maniacs.

There in the midst of the pandemonium, Bishop Rudd stood on one side, and David Kent on the other, and between them was Crete Colton, safe for the moment from the rush of those whose fear of self hurt was driving them to worse. Instinctively, the girl's arms were about one of the men—it was Rudd. For the space of a second or two they stood, Crete making no move or outcry, while the men warded off the rush.

Then into the compact human mass about them bolted the manager of the Bonanza Irrigation Company, a man gone mad with fear for himself. And seeing him and his madness, the little Bishop did that which neither Crete Colton nor David Kent ever forgot.

In one fierce swift flash the little man was at the big one and had him out of the crowd where he was smashing for his own life and imperiling a score of others; had him out, gasping, frothing, purple with rage and fear; out, on his back, literally thrown into a corner.

Quicker than words was it all. So sudden, so unexpected, so audacious that it seized the attention of those close at hand, and so for a moment saved them from themselves and their fear. Bishop Rudd *had their attention*. And the little Bishop seized his opportunity.

"*God damn cowards to hell!*"

He was on a bench. A dozen regarded him

open-mouthed. The words shocked them, held them astounded, fascinated.

"*I say God damn cowards all to hell!*"

The little Bishop spoke not loudly, but the voice of him was cool, penetrating, bell-like. And all at once the group which heard and noted enlarged, and suddenly the magnetic interest somehow spread and others in the swirling human whirlpool, more distant, turned to see the nature of this new storm center, and saw and heard him, and their minds became struck with the stupendous phenomenon of a Bishop blaspheming so mightily.

Then someone laughed.

In six seconds the panic was over. The incipient fire was out, and shamefacedly those who had smothered it by their very impact drew apart.

"Thank God for our Bishop," said the mother of the little baby. "Amen" echoed a burly rancher, who a minute before had been crazy with unreasoning fear.

"An' a while ago he was a-praying against *profanity*," muttered Dad Trumble, with moist-eyed approval. "The bygoddest Bishop ever I see."

CHAPTER XII

POOR LITTLE LUCY

"It's the best way of travelin' there is," declared Dad Trumble, lighting his first pipe of the day as he crooked one stubby leg around the saddle horn to face Rudd the more comfortably. "It's the acumen of comfort, as they say. This way we can go jest where we like 'thout being bound by roads and trails, and the whole blame shebang's right there on the pack-horse when it comes to eatin' an' sleepin'. Yer can't beat it!"

Behind Trumble and the Bishop rode Kent, he having volunteered to lead the pack-horse on this first stretch of their vacation journey, which, to the satisfaction of all three, had been extemporized a few days after the settlers' meeting.

By sun-up they were well out of town, abandoning the dusty road for the needle-carpeted floor of the forest, with the copper-colored trunks of the great trees on either hand, massive pillars lining marvelous nature-made aisles. Here and there a blaze, gashed in the thick alligator-like bark of the pines, marked the trail which was to lead them up into the mountains.

The sheep had not yet reached the forest reserves, so the bunch grass still showed brownish green, the manzanita, chemise, and snowbush retained their foliage, and the broad parklike reaches beneath the trees were unsullied. A fortnight later, when the herders drove their wooly bands to the upland summer pastures, while bobtailed dogs ran hither and thither doing the bidding of their Basque masters, and the whole forest was a welter of dust and a babel of witless bleating, the perfection of the pinelands would be banished.

But in June, when the last spring showers were gratefully fresh in memory and the sheep had not yet come from their winter feeding grounds in the alfalfa valleys to the east and north, the timbered country was perfection. The tree trunks stood gold and brown and copper. Olive green the lofty needles glinted and above their transparent pavilion glowed a brillant sky of pure blue, with never a cloud to mar its infinite depth. The glossy lacquered leaves of the manzanita danced in the sunbeams, reflecting their rays like myriad tiny mirrors. The air was an elixir of the very love of life; perfume of pines, pleasant tang of neighbor snowfields, rareness of oxygen bracingly thin with goodly altitude, all made a blend whose breathing was enviable intoxication.

"It's a sacrilege to smoke," said the Bishop, his lips smilingly encircling the stem of a battered corncob.

"And a sacrifice not to!" Kent added.

They nooned at the shady edge of a little meadow, where a spring bubbled capriciously from under the sod. The horses rolled and munched their fill, while the men ate and smoked and then resaddled.

The big pines gave way to scrubby timber, mostly thickets of "black jack" or lodgepole pine, poor scrawny stuff clustering together so closely that there was no passage other than the cut-out trail. Then all at once, coming out upon a ridge top, they looked across a gray barren upland valley where a forest fire had left the tragic scar which woodmen call a burn. Beyond the valley were towsled hills, the real foothills, with the great pile of the Chief with its gleaming snowfields towering seemingly just above them.

A leisurely afternoon they made of it, ending early at Little Lake, where the grass was green and high for the horses and the trout displayed a healthy interest in the flies which ever and anon met swift disaster as they flitted too carelessly across the quiet water.

"There isn't the remotest doubt," said Rudd that evening as he removed the backbone of his fifth fish, "that Dad is the finest trout cooker extant."

Kent, equally busy as a trencherman, agreed heartily.

"And speaking of trout, this feed wouldn't be complete without a fish story. Dad has a world beater . . . tell it to the Bishop, Dad."

Dad Trumble eyed the young man coolly.

"*Fish* stories, *as sich*," he opined, "are *one* thing . . . an' gospel truth is another."

"I take it this one has a gospel guarantee then," offered the Bishop unsanctimoniously. "For my part I always believe fish stories anyway . . . especially if they're good ones."

"Like that Jonah whopper?" Dad put in with a mischievous twinkle.

Rudd nodded good-naturedly; he sought no ecclesiastical argument.

"Wall," the story-teller started, with a thoughtful pull on his pipe, "th' first year I came to Farewell—that was way back yonder almost before th' lavy flows had cooled down—I caught a most awfully nice healthy lookin' trout jes' below the big eddy where th' power dam's now. He was sich a right smart appearin' fish I didn't have the heart to kill him so I packed him home careful as could be an' rigged up a big pan o' water for him. At fust he seemed as content and cosy as a worm on a wet morning."

The old man puffed his pipe seriously, his face clouding with the awakened memory of that piscatorial tragedy.

"But he was young, that trout . . . th' boys called him Lucy, although she really was a he . . . there's something so *feminine*-like about a real gentle affectionate fish, ye jes' can't help of using girl cognobles . . . perhaps you've noticed that?"

Poor Little Lucy

The Bishop acquiesced. "Of course—heaven bless the ladies!"

"Lucy was young an' pert, an' purty soon she seemed to sort o' tire of her restricted district, so ter speak. At least, she got po'ful impatient for more room to move around in, like as if she craved to see something of the world, same as lots o' innocent young things." Dad blew his nose vehemently. "An' she fretted around so she—that is, *he*—sloshed all the water out of the pan most every day. At first I kept filling it up until I began to notice Lucy seemed to enjoy himself most when he was clean out of water. Wall, sir, would you believe it, that bygod fish got ter living so much *out* of water that pretty soon he jes' naturally couldn't stand the *feel* of wet on him at all. Onct, when he got rained on good and proper, he took down with a most alarmin' chill . . . had ter keep him by the stove for a week before he properly got over it. Breathe? Mos' absolutely he could breathe . . . jes' th' same's me or you. It's all a matter of habit, breathin' is, jes' like whisky or politicks . . . yer kin get used to most any brand if yer try."

"I suppose Lucy lived to a ripe and happy old age?" asked the Bishop.

"I reckon not," Dad replied, again using his veteran bandanna generously. "It's a plumb sorrowful yarn. Yer see, Bish, little Lucy an' I got ter be th' best kind o' pals . . . me havin' no folks an' batchin' that way. As he got bigger an' more aklemated, as it were, that bygod friendly little cuss'd follow me all around like a dog. How? Why, ain't yer never seen a fish *flop?* Lucy was the prizedest spryest flopper ever I set eyes on, an' like the breathin', the more he practiced the abler he got. Of'entimes I'd take him up town in my pocket to do little tricks for the boys on Jeb Watterson's counter.... But mostly when I went away I'd leave Lucy in the cabin, com'forble an' cosy on my bunk."

Silence.

The narrator knocked the ashes from his pipe.

"Then one day I come away in a hurry an' forgot to close th' door..."

Again silence, still more tragic.

"Well?"

"Well," echoed Dad with a heartfelt sigh, "that was th' ruination of Lucy. In them days there was a big foot-log 'cross th' river jes' in front of my shack. When I was most over it, hurrying to town, I heard a sort o' familiar flip-flop behind me... an' there was Lucy jes' a bouncing along down the trail from the door to t'other end o' th' log. I hollered fer him to go back but he jes' up and waved that cute spotted tail o' his, contrary wise, 'smuch as ter say, 'No, yer don't go off and leave me, Ol' Timer'... that there Lucy was the faithfullest, affectionest critter that ever was in these parts... and *brains*"... he paused, pondering Lucy's mental attributes ... "why, he had brains all over his body!"

Another pause, to soothe the pains of memory refreshed. "Soon's I see Lucy wouldn't go home I started back 'cross th' log to head him off. But he was floppin' too fast . . . he beat me to the log an' started ker-flippin' out along it to meet me, jes' as smilin' an' happy as ever any fish in the world. Then all to 'onct" . . . the old man's voice faltered, as he turned away his head . . . "all to onct little Lucy caught his left fore fin in a sliver and lost his balance. . . . There he tetered for th' time it'd take to snap yer finger, sort o' quivering on th' edge of the log, six feet above the rough water . . . then, jes' as I got there an' was reachin' down to save him . . . he plumb lost his grip an' over he went!"

Dad blew his nose again.

"The boys found him where he drifted up on the sand below the riffle . . . an' we buried him . . . proper . . ."

"Why, surely he could swim . . ." began the Bishop.

"Not Lucy . . . he'd forgotten all about water . . . *poor lil' Lucy drowned!*"

CHAPTER XIII

LOST LAKE

WITH leisurely journeying they came the next afternoon to the crest of a bare ridge at the far side of Wickiup Flat whence they looked down upon the curious country surrounding Lost Lake. Persistent snow patches covered the trail here and there despite the warming summer suns, and close at hand greater fields of snow projected down among the barren moraines and scattered tamarack trees.

While the other members of the party regarded the widespreading view before them, Dad Trumble repaired a cairn of stones marking the trail, mishandled by winter storms.

"Why the monument?" Kent asked.

Trumble reinforced the base of the cairn with a heavy rock and wedged a gnarled bit of tamarack branch, whitely weather beaten, into the top of the pile, so that it stood out conspicuously.

"In Noo York I reckon they label the bygod streets, don't they?" was his laconic rejoinder.

Kent, getting the point, nodded.

"Ye see, Dave, this here avenoo we're on is

Lost Lake 121

pretty important—leastwise, it used to be. It's the main route of the Ringo Trail which crosses the mountains from Farewell to the Valley. In the old days when everything east of the divide moved on horseback, it was the one big way over to the Welcome River country. An' so" . . . Dad, having given the cairn a finishing touch, swung into his saddle . . . "I mos' always try to help keep the old trail well marked. In summer it's easy enough when you can see the landmarks, an' it's always plain sailing in the timber with the blazes on the trees. But give her a foot of snow here near the top, an' a squall so thick ye can't see the hosses' ears, an' the chances of getting lost and freezing up tight is elegant."

From their vantage point they all looked at the lake below them, and its queer environs. Seemingly a satanic force had played fast and loose with the great piles of fire-glazed rock round about. The lake itself was mounted like a gem in a setting of emerald meadow, a tiny gayly colored parkplace hemmed in by gray talus slopes and fantastic heaps of rock, which seemed to have been shot out from the side of the Chief, crashing down about it in million-tonned avalanches. Here and there huge bowlders sprawled in the grassy field at the water's edge, with purple lupin and the tawny Indian paintbrush flower clustering beside them.

Lost Lake, encompassed by the mountains, lay at the very top of the divide, or, at least, at the summit of the pass where the Ringo Trail found a way across the range. From it a deep quick stream started boldly westward through the grassy meadow, swirled surprisedly around and over some vagrant bowlders, outposts of the main avalanche and centuries ago worn glassy smooth by the diligent waters, and then, foaming bravely, dashed into the maelstrom of rocks contesting further passage. Here an arm of talus, spilling down from the Chief, reached out across the stream, barring its progress. The waters gurgled and fought and sighed, and then all at once disappeared through cracks and caverns into the shadow lands below.

That evening, when the Bishop had taken the axe and gone beyond the circle of firelight in search of more boughs for his bed, Kent sought information from Dad Trumble.

"Most of that settlers' meeting was a rank puzzle to me," he offered encouragingly.

"Umph!"

"I'd like to know what's behind it all."

"Cats has been killed by it," the old man remarked dryly.

"Oh, yes, I know curiosity sometimes is fatal," laughed Kent, "but what did you mean when you said there wasn't enough water in Welcome River to care for the South Canal segregation as well as the original contract holders?"

"I meant—" the older man hesitated. "I meant just what I said. There ain't enough water, and there never will be until someone pulls off another one of those blamed miracles."

"But the report . . . Failing's engineers say there's plenty of water."

"Report hell! What's a report 'tween friends?" grunted Dad. "It's this way, an' you may as well know it now as later. That engineer's report is all bunk . . . plain skuldugery of the rankest sort. Failing brought a kid glove boy out from the a-feet East ter do th' work, and he found right soon there wasn't more than 1800 second feet of water on the average. Now, that's just about what's needed for the present segregation."

"How do you know all this?"

"The Lord rewards virtoo, 1 'spose. Anyway, He let me catch them scalawags with an extra ace tucked in their sleeve. It's this way. That summer when they had the engineering gang out I went along as cook. We started in up at the meadows, and worked all the way down to Farewell with measurements and surveys. You see, there never had been any reg'lar dope kept on the river before. That was when they first cooked up the plan for the new South Canal unit, and they wanted to prove that there was water enough to handle it. Well, they proved it right enough. Only the Lord, as I've remarked, was good and let me in on the secret."

Dad puffed his pipe and spat largely into the fire.

"One night we was campin' at Piney Falls, ten

miles above Farewell. From the down-in-the-mouth worrit look of young Welton—that's the boss engineer, you know—I suspicioned something was plumb wrong. About mess time along comes Jim Failing in his team, looking as if he'd lost his last friend . . . only I don't 'spose he ever did have a reg'lar friend, nohow. When grub was through Failing and Welton got out th' dope sheets an' maps all over the tables, messing up my new oilcloth something scandalous. Then they went to talking, sort of low voiced, to match their spirits, which certainly was about at zero. And—oh, well, in course it wasn't *egzakly* accordin' ter Doyle, but I stuck tight in the cooktent, which was dark so they didn't think no one was there. Then they got a bit excited and loosened up their language so's I heard it all easy as snaggin' fish. Th' upshoot was that Welton agreed to doctor the records. That night they did an awful lot more than the Lord could get away with, for they boosted old Welcome River about a thousand second feet, which was generous of 'em. I heard the whole shebang, and saw a deal of it. But I never let on a whimper; sort of thought it'd be best to wait for the bygod uppertuned moment, as the feller said."

Kent, wondering why the fraud had never been discovered, asked Dad if it were not true that stations were maintained to measure and record the flow of Welcome River. And the old man told him that was true enough, reminding him, however, that it was Failing himself who did the measuring at the rapids just above Farewell and one of his men at the up-river station. As for the Government observer twelve miles downstream at Eagle Ferry, it was a well-known local phenomenon that almost a third of the flow was supposed to vanish between Farewell and there, presumably through subterranean fissures, just as a portion of the river above Farewell actually disappeared in the lava fields.

"Why don't you tell the whole dirty business?"

"Can't." Dad's brief word cut short the excursion of Kent's puzzled mind. "I jest naturally can't . . . 'twould break her all up."

The girl again! Unfathomably she seemed to bob up as a vital factor in all the larger complexities of the little world into whose entanglements he had plunged.

"Who is this Welton, anyway?"

"He's from the East . . . but it shouldn't be held against him," replied Dad, with a quizzical smile. "Friend of Failing's backers, I understan'. A purty good highbrow engineer, too, and fair to middlin' ter look at—which fact the bygod coot seems to savvy. When it comes ter dollin' up there ain't a Christmas tree as can touch him."

"But what has he to do with Miss Colton?"

Dad Trumble regarded the fire silently, his eyes for once without their twinkle.

"Girls," said he, "is foolish . . . mostly.

About this crooked report matter, why, I jest naturally had to tell someone, so I told her, way back—I mos' generally do tell her, yer see." The old man smiled softly. "An' then if she didn't flamboozle her old bygod Dad by up an' tellin' me —but say, David, secrets is secrets."

Thereat the old man straightened to the full majesty of his five feet four inches, loosed a magnificent flurry of sparks from the back log with a deft kick, and hallooed to the Bishop.

Shortly Rudd returned, burdened with balsam boughs.

"Say, Dad, I hope retribution for your sins doesn't overtake you to-night in the shape of an earthquake, for there's an avalanche hanging up there just waiting for a word of encouragement."

"I'm in good company if it's coming!" Dad replied with a grin, spreading his blankets, and the others squirmed into their sleeping bags.

While the dying fire dwindled and the stars gleamed the brighter, David Kent lay cozily, his dreams more of the day than of the night. His experiences since casting in his fortunes with Farewell rehearsed before his mind, and all the details of these Oregon days marshaled themselves in retrospect, as clear and sharp as the night air itself. Curiously, Kent's thoughts were less and less of his own problems. True, Valentine, a joyous ultimate promise, served always as a mental background; his was a pilgrimage, its goal attainment of the beautiful gray girl. But as he lay beneath the night sky, consciously reveling in his aloneness, it was the problems of his new friends which most concerned him.

Out from the purple plush overhead the legionary stars smiled intimately. The clean fragrance of dirt and grass clung close to his earthy bed, and the frosty nip of the ageing night made that blanketed couch seem secure and warm beyond belief. From the meadow where the horses browsed there came at lessening intervals the thud of their hobbled forefeet as they moved from one grazing ground to another. As their appetites slaked these predatory excursions waned, until finally even the bell of Lazy Jake, the packhorse, ceased to tinkle. Persistent through this ultimate calm sounded the swirl of the running water where Lost Lake overflowed in the short-lived stream.

"So there isn't enough water in Welcome River," he mused. "If they ever do get a square report that'll be discovered and the South Canal scheme goes to blazes." He realized well enough the result meant no fresh funds from the new unit to put the old in workable shape and save the settlers. A crash must come. And that would mean the canals left as they were, leaking and inadequate; no more laterals to lead the water to the lands of those who had contracted for it; remote settlers left to their fate, waterless, with next to no recourse, with none of the expected mortgage-lifting crops obtainable and their little capital already devoured by initial payments—investment small enough, perhaps, reckoned in dollars, but enormously large in the bitter currency of wasted years and shattered hopes.

If only there were some miraculous cure for the sick project, some neglected lever upon Failing, some desperate hold whereby he could be strangled into full justice for his settlers, some untried opportunity to pry loose the contents of conservative moneybags! And the key of it all, Kent saw clearly, was with the river itself—if the fatal lack of water could be remedied!

Quiet indeed it was; too quiet even to think, Kent felt, as he tried to ponder. Only the sound of the running water disturbed the overwhelming hush, a babbling, monotonous undertone. Almost, it seemed to him, there were intelligible words in the everlasting music of the stream. "Find—us—if—you—can . . . find—us—if—you—can . . . find—us—if—you—can—" over and over, over and over in his mind the words ran, to the tune of the running water. There seemed an insolence in the measured message—a subtle invitation—a veritable challenge. . . .

All at once Kent sat up straight beneath the stars. For a full minute he was silent, his brain racing. Then a wild yell, triumphant, joyous, surged into the silent night. The startled horses snorted and charged away.

"Whasmatter? A rattler?" The Little Bishop's voice was anxious.

But Kent only laughed—laughed until the sleeping bag fell away from his shoulders.

"A *hell* of a joke!" Dad snapped, rubbing his eyes. He had expected nothing less than a marauding bear. "I suppose," he continued with sour facetiousness, "you dreamed of a bygod feather bed and woke us up to hear about it?"

"What is it, Kent?" Rudd looked a bit alarmed.

The disturber of sleep assumed a serious air.

"Nothing much," said he, mildly. "Only I've found enough water for all the settlers——"

"Got it with you?" Dad interrupted. Neither practical jokes nor dreams appealed to him at that time of night.

"No, Dad. Not right here . . . but it's not far away."

"Remember, the day of miracles is past," admonished the Bishop.

But the young man smiled complacently.

"Watch me!"

CHAPTER XIV

NEWS EXTRAORDINARY

"AND did you file on the water?"

"No, I didn't file. In the first place, there wasn't time, and secondly, it is hardly necessary yet."

"Well, tell me about it if you care to." Pharaoh was frankly interested.

"There is nothing to it . . . absolutely nothing!" Kent spoke with enthused conviction. "All I have to do is to cork up the western outlet and raise the level of the lake a bit, and then the overflow will come this way, just as it did a few hundred years ago."

Pharaoh, his big brow puckered more thoughtfully than ever, asked how much water the overflow contained.

"I asked Rudd and Dad, at different times. The Bishop estimated five hundred second feet—he had some engineering training, you know. Dad said over six hundred. Anyway, there's an extraordinary lot of water boiling out of the lake, what with the drainage from the everlasting snow on the Chief and the springs which force up from the bottom."

News Extraordinary

"Well, say there was five hundred feet. That would be all very nice if you could get it to Welcome River, but how much do you 'spose that would cost, and how much would be lost on the way?"

"I went into that a bit with Rudd . . ."

"Oh, the Bishop knows, does he?"

"Yes . . . and the Church is about the only institution I'd trust with the secret—unless it's the *Pioneer!*" laughed Kent. "Rudd and I did a bit of rough reconnoisance work, and it looks as if all we'd have to do would be to spill the Lost Lake overflow down from its meadow, and gravitation would attend to the rest. There's an old natural channel which winds around all the way to Little Lake, and the spring overflow of Little Lake already goes into Welcome River although at present it doesn't amount to anything. In other words," the young man juggled mountain lakes with humorous abandon, "I propose to dump Lost Lake into Welcome River!"

"Remember about Man proposing and the Lord disposing!" Pharaoh cautioned. "But even if it was all clear sailing you'll have to get your water rights first, and then comes the real work and the right of way which . . ."

"It's all through the Forest Reserve . . . the right of way question is easy. As for the other . . ."

Pharaoh guessed what was in his mind.

"Cash?"

Kent nodded.

"Got any?"

"Yes . . . and no!" He *had* some money, truly enough, but his agreement with Valentine forbade his touching it during this trial year.

"Well, you better find out whether you have or you haven't. As for me,"—the editor scratched his thatched dome quizzically,—"I don't generally have any trouble determining whether I'm a millionaire or a pauper—there's no 'yes-an'-no' to that, even for the assessor. Howsoever" . . . he moved off toward the back shop . . . "there's a bit of a job to be set up, and I'll thank you to read the proofs while I get at the cases."

On Pharaoh's littered desk, flanked on one side by a blue Department of Agriculture report (dealing with the Boll Weevil in Louisiana) and on the other by a neat pyramid of seed packages distributed by a provident Congressman, there lay the planer proofs of that week's edition. Kent took up the first of these and immediately his eye encountered an item under a one-line head which banished further thoughts of labor for that day.

"Capitalist Coming." That was the headline.

"Accompanied by Max Welton, his engineer, and by his daughter, Miss Valentine, Alton Pennoyer, a capitalist of New York, arrived last night." Kent rubbed his eyes, glancing up as if half expecting to see the Pennoyers. Then he remembered that this item was to appear in the *Pioneer* of Wednesday, and this was Tuesday;

News Extraordinary

so the "last night" of the proof actually meant that very evening.

"To-night! Of all the everlasting . . ."

But Kent's amazed exclamation tapered off into a gurgle. The reason for the Pennoyers' advent to Farewell was apparent enough in the words of the proof—words that fairly rose up from the smudgy paper and smote him with sudden and complete confusion.

"Mr. Pennoyer is one of the largest stockholders in the Bonanza Irrigation Company, and is visiting the project not only to see his own investment at first hand, but also as the representative of a group of eastern gentlemen who, it is understood, control the company. According to Manager Failing, the party will remain in Farewell a week or more. Speaking of this country and its prospects, Mr. Pennoyer said—" the inky mourning band of an inverted slug at that point, followed by the words "Statement to kom," indicated that Editor Jones had not deemed it expedient to indite Mr. Pennoyer's utterances for him in advance of their enunciation.

For thirty long slow seconds the cogs of Kent's brain refused to mesh.

Then they flew together and the mechanism rushed madly on while a mental moving picture of all the distressing dilemmas of the new situation whirled through his head until it was hot and his hands were cold and that part of his stomach which authors term the pit became unhappily numb.

For here he had blundered face to face with the astounding fact that Valentine's father was the financial angel of the Bonanza Company and undoubtedly the guiding accomplice of its manager; and here was he plotting war upon that company and pledged to the cause of the settlers in their struggle against the machinations of Failing—here he stood, indeed, well branded as a thorn in the side of those who conducted and those who financed the B. I. C.

"*Hell!*" said he, whole-souledly.

A pretty development, he thought, in this Quixotic cross-continent quest of success—the sort of success which this very father of Valentine demanded. Not simply a development, but probably enough the very end of it. Surely so, indeed, unless he changed his course . . . and there his racing mind slowed down to consider the new notion. . . . Right-about-face! Why not? . . . It had been done before, and with less reason. . . . It would be easy . . . very, very easy . . . infinitely easier than persisting in the present vexatious path. . . . After all, why not?

Dust and desert and poverty; struggle and disappointment and failure. As Kent rehearsed it all his spirits sank lower and lower. For the settlers and the town the future seemed to him unutterably dark; for himself he foresaw complications which seemingly could have no other ending than speedy ruin of all his cherished desires and plans.

"What's wrong?" asked the lean editor, returning from the shop.

"Everything."

With the frankness of a troubled mind, he started to pour forth his woes, but the story was scarcely commenced when the door of the *Pioneer's* office opened upon Crete Colton. There was dust upon her shoulders and on the battered hat which carelessly held captive the mass of pale hair; while the smile of the blue sky itself seemed in her frank eyes and the brown of the sun-kissed land reflected in the tan of her cheeks.

"'Morning, folks!" Then, catching the sober look of the two men, the ample mouth pulled down at the corners mock-dolorously. "Oh, excuse me. Where's the corpse?"

Without waiting for a reply she dropped into Pharaoh's chair, assuming an air of sanctimonious sympathy. "Do you object to another mourner?"

"No, indeed," Kent laughed. "We're glad to have you. And as to the corpse, I'm in the heavy rôle myself. At least," he stated more exactly, "I will be soon enough . . . probably."

"Oh . . . 'soon enough . . . probably.' That's odd. It sounds like a sacrifice with the hero inclined to bolt at the last minute and disappoint an expectant audience. As for me" . . . Crete pouted gravely . . . "I insist upon getting the act as advertised. No rain checks."

"But you see I never contracted anything," Kent replied.

"Then there's nothing for you to lose."

"No . . . nothing. Nothing, that is, unless" . . . the young man hesitated . . . "unless—oh, well, unless I go ahead." He ended ambiguously.

Something of his meaning, of what lay behind his words, reached Crete. Walking to the window she looked out upon the dismal dustiness, the parched plains and the vacant lots of the city-to-be whose dreams had not come true. Beyond all this she could see the waterless lands of the segregation, the gray sagebrush plains, the fences and shacks of the settlers, the men working on their ditches and the women toiling with their cookstoves and their babies. And still beyond, the impelling background of all the rough new country in the making, the force that spurred forward all the best elements of its pioneering, there was clear to Crete Colton the ultimate end and reward of it all—green turf, plowed fields, happy homes, and contented communities. Her eyes, too, saw the splendid mountains; and they seemed a beckoning promise of the future.

"Are you going ahead . . . or back?" The girl spoke quietly.

"Ahead or back?" Kent repeated lamely, "What do you mean?"

Turning from the window, she faced him squarely.

"You know well enough." There was weariness and disappointment in her tone. "There's a big man's work here—the work of pioneers in any new country. You know what there is to be done, and you know that women can't do it all —even with the help of dear Pharaoh here. Providence or a guilty conscience or something—we don't care what," she smiled through the mistiness that gathered as her words poured forth, "brought you to deliver us, a Daniel . . ."

"No, a David, as it happens!" he broke in.

"Well, David, then . . . you've come to the valley for battle and already the giant has challenged you. You, David Kent, are the only one among us who dare answer that challenge. Take your five stones, David, and smite Goliath's brazen helmet . . ."

"He's got plenty of brass, God knows," growled Kent.

"And if you don't" . . . she hesitated . . . "well, if you fail us Goliath will crush us all . . ."

She was standing straight now, beside the window, its light full upon her firm face, and her blue eyes resolutely upon his. "So it's really David's move . . . and what will David Kent do? Go forth and fight or quit? You know just what I meant when I asked if you are going ahead or back . . . ahead into trouble, probably with no profit to yourself . . . or back to your own country and your own people . . . back to comfort and refinement, to a land where folks believe there isn't such a thing as pioneering to-day outside of the movies."

Pharaoh was genuinely troubled. It seemed

preposterous to him for Crete to lecture Kent as she was doing; had not he just told him of his plans with Lost Lake—plans which, if successful, would solve the whole problem and bring the Irrigation Company to terms?

"Why, Crete," the editor expostulated mildly, "I can't make out what you're driving at. You talk as if Mr. Kent had thrown up the sponge."

"Well, hasn't he? Haven't you, Mr. Kent?"

For the seconds in which Kent faced Crete Colton silently, poor Pharaoh's heart sank. Then his young assistant shook his head.

"Of course he hasn't!" Pharaoh ejaculated, infinitely relieved. With an air of triumph, he continued: "The truth is, Crete, Kent here has the company crowd backed off the map . . . he's got those Philistines with their tails between their legs."

Then the editor proceeded impetuously to confide to Crete Colton what Kent had just told him. "And it's perfectly feasible," he wound up in a glow of enthusiasm. "All that's necessary is to get the filings safely made and then with that stick over his head it won't be hard to make Failing come to terms—he'll have to contract to use all the South Canal profits on the old segregation, eh, Kent?"

"No more contracts. A bird in the hand is worth a flock in the sagebrush. Failing won't get that water, and the chance that goes with it to clean up on the new unit, unless he first makes the present settlers whole, and delivers water to every acre of sold land."

"Oh!" said Miss Colton, and that was all.

"How much water were *you* short last year, Crete?" asked Pharaoh.

"Another two days of the lateral would have saved the crop. But I let the Sorensons on the ditch below me have the water then—all their alfalfa depended upon it, and with four children and a mortgage they seemed to need it worse than I did. The new people at the end of the ditch burned up entirely." She considered that tragedy thoughtfully. "They were new last year and really didn't have much in crops, but it broke them anyway. They went back to Wisconsin."

"Will it be any better this year, as matters stand?" Kent asked.

"No, probably not. The ditches are the same size but a little more leaky. They haven't spent any money repairing them—the company declares there isn't any more money. Down at the Capitol the Land Board says there's nothing it can do to force the company—the old story of getting blood from a turnip. But it doesn't make much difference to me . . . personally, that is," she corrected herself with a wry little smile; "even if there was oodles of water I couldn't run the ranch next season." She studied one tanned wrist thoughtfully. "I'm broke. . . dead broke!"

"As bad as that?"

She nodded.

"And which way are *you* going . . . ahead or back?"

He put her own query to her gently.

"Oh, I'm . . . I'm stationary."

"It seems to me," he said after a pause, "that you are the one really best qualified as a mourner, at least so far as logical reasons for mournfulness go. . . . Although somehow" . . . he looked with frank admiration at the girl's sunny face . . . "you never would fill the bill very well, professionally speaking."

"The Lord gave me a sense of humor, anyway," she replied. "That helps."

"I reckon He overlooked me when it came to dishing out that asset!" Pharaoh exclaimed with a wry smile. "The situation doesn't strike me as especially *damned* funny!"

"Well, if the truth must be told, I wouldn't call you a court jester," said Kent good-naturedly.

The girl, seeing deeper into his mood, sensed something radically wrong.

"We've all gone on the mourners' bench and confessed," said she. "It's your turn now, Pharaoh."

And Pharaoh, encouraged, told what he had been withholding from Kent, hesitating, in his inherent kindliness, to so soon oppress the high spirits of the returned vacationist with his own worries. Failing had served notice that unless the *Pioneer* forthwith got in line approving the South Canal unit there would be no more advertising and no more job work.

"So he wants you to boost the new segregation?" The girl's cool voice broke the silence.

"Yes. He says one good issue of the *Pioneer* telling all about it—the way he sees it, of course —would settle the matter. He's to have maps drawn and plates made and . . . and" . . . the distressed editor actually choked . . . "*he's to write it all himself*. There's to be a big edition . . . a thousand extra copies. With that—says Failing—he can put the deal over. No one much gets out of here to the Capitol. .'. ."

"Because they haven't the price," muttered Kent bitterly.

"So the folks down there'll take the *Pioneer* about at par—they'll believe it says what the people up here think. 'An independent expression of the desires of the community' is what he calls it . . . *independent* . . . my God!" After a minute of silence he continued wearily: "He's reasonably decent on the money end. We owe him five hundred dollars on the land and we're to get a receipt for this, and deed, when it is delivered."

"It?" The girl's voice sounded very far away.

"The special edition . . . the boost for the South Canal scheme."

"Then you're going to . . ."

Pharaoh nodded.

"It's the only thing to do. It's a losing fight . . . there's no use bucking this . . . this octopus. Oh yes, I know they're a measly lot; a few strong men could clean them up . . . but that takes money . . . God! how many things take money! And we're like you Crete, only worse . . . without the company business the *Pioneer*'d go to smash in a month . . . we'll have to eat out of it's hand. After all" . . . his voice was more resolute, but there was no ring of conviction in the words . . . "this is simply a matter of business . . . strictly dollars and cents. It's a chance to make a good turn."

"A matter of business!" thought Kent to himself. For a space he pondered unpleasantly and then said aloud to Pharaoh: "What will the people say?"

"Just what I'd say in their place . . . they'll damn me from Hell to breakfast. But I won't care . . . that is, not particularly. What they think of me won't hurt the paper, anyway, because . . . because . . . oh, well, you folks may as well know the whole thing. . . . *I'm going to sell the Pioneer!*"

Kent and Crete received the announcement in astonished silence.

"Failing is giving me an agreement to buy the paper, if I want to sell within ninety days. It's a handsome price—four thousand dollars—more than the plant is really worth and enough to pay off everything and leave us in the clear."

Crete Colton drew an envelope from the pocket of her mackinaw.

"Well, Pharaoh," said she quietly, "it looks

News Extraordinary 143

as if 'retreat' had sounded. A little while ago I asked Mr. Kent whether it was ahead or back with him—he evidently being in a cold funk on the country." Despite the passing smile, the girl's caustic tone cut. "As this seems to have developed into an epidemic of confessions I might as well make mine, too. This," she held the letter in her brown hand, "this is an offer to teach in Seattle—the best I ever had."

Kent, beside the window, caught the full glint of sunshine upon the mountain flanks, and his spirit responded. After all, he had at least found himself in time to prevent an irreparable break with Valentine's father; Pharaoh would attain a measure of financial competency; and lastly, Crete Colton, the enigma of the play behind whose scenes he had chanced, was afforded a pleasant opportunity to shake the dust of Oregon from her feet, together with her present troubles. The clouds seemed all at once lined with silver.

But something seen just then through the window banished every other thought.

"Good Lord! Here's the stage!" And with that David Kent bolted from the office.

CHAPTER XV

ARRIVAL UNEXPECTED

"WELL, I suppose I'll have to let you," Alton Pennoyer had begrudgingly conceded when Valentine pressed her desire to accompany him on the western trip.

"And, Dads," continued Valentine, after registering her appreciation, "there's another favor. No . . . no!" she laughingly captured her father's hands, raised in mock surrender, "it isn't money . . . although of course I *will* need some. . . . It's just that I want you to promise not to tell anyone out there I'm going with you."

"Out there? What do you mean, my dear?"

"At Farewell."

"Umph! I'd almost forgotten. Young Kent is there, eh? So that's the reason for this sudden interest in your poor old Dad."

Pennoyer studied his daughter thoughtfully.

"What about this fellow anyway, Val?"

"Nothing especial . . . nothing definite, anyway," she replied, her gray eyes returning his glance.

"Does he know you're coming?"

"No. And I don't want him to."

"Why?"

"Oh, I'd just like to happen in and see how he really is getting along. From his letters . . ."

"Then he writes to you?"

"Of course. Why not?"

Pennoyer disregarded the question.

"You remember, Dads, how he went out there—wanted to make good and all that . . . show me he could succeed on his own hook. He selected Farewell because Bishop Rudd talked so much about it. At the time I didn't know you had any interest there and since I discovered it I've never told Da—Mr. Kent. You were sort of mean not to let us know . . . you might have helped him."

Pennoyer smiled at the memory of his little deception.

"No," said he, "it wasn't mean. He wanted to stand on his own feet and I didn't feel like supplying crutches. In fact," he chuckled dryly, "if my information is correct he's not only on his feet but on my toes as well!"

"How, Dads?"

"Oh, the young fool's taken up with a bunch of anarchist settlers who don't understand that investors have any rights and that dividends must be paid—if they're not, development stops short." Conversationally sidetracked to a business subject Pennoyer's voice hardened. "I've sunk a lot of good money out there and things haven't gone well—no profits and poor prospects of any. Instead, they want me to dump more cash into the damned scheme. The settlers aren't satisfied with what they have and demand all sorts of expensive improvements. They don't ask—they demand! As if they didn't owe us everything!"

"But what has Mr. Kent to do with it?" Valentine asked mildly.

"Nothing—and a good deal. It's absolutely none of his business as he doesn't own an acre or a share of stock. But somehow he's got tangled up with the settlers. According to Failing, the manager, he's in a fair way to raise the regular devil by stirring up a lot of adverse publicity in connection with a new deal we're launching."

Thereupon handsome, elderly Alton Pennoyer, gray of mustache and hair, told handsome young Valentine Pennoyer the main facts of the little universe where irrigation was so nearly the beginning and ending of all things. He told it from his own standpoint, of course, which was precisely that of countless thousands of well-fed landlords discussing the unreasonable demands of their tenants.

He was past the ripeness of middle age, and she was scarce full bloomed; the girl was tall and slender, and the man substantially stocky. But the same imperiousness was written in the clean-cut lines of the two faces, the same shrewdness in the cool eyes, the same quick blood richly colored the old and the young cheeks, and the same something of selfish determination lurked about the

Arrival Unexpected 147

two mouths. Father and daughter were creditable examples of American commercial aristocracy whose inalienable birthrights are competence and prosperity.

Valentine may not have understood all the details of her father's exposition of the affairs of the Bonanza Irrigation Company, but certain salient features she did grasp. Among them was the fact that if the South Canal unit could be launched Alton Pennoyer was certain of a handsome profit, whereas if it were blocked the company seemed fated to flounder further in a deepening mire of debt and difficulty. And crowning it all was the startling realization that her own would-be fiancé was the very one whose endeavors, if persisted in, might defeat her parent's efforts.

"It's all Dads' fault . . . every bit of it!" she pouted at her mirror that evening, uncontradicted. If he had only told her, or David, of his interest in the Irrigation Company there would have been no trouble.

By the time she was ready for bed she had evolved a plan. It was ridiculously simple; she would call David off and make him work with her father instead of against him—provided Alton Pennoyer placed his approval upon a certain life contract which she conceded might as well be entered into now as at any later time between herself and David Kent. It was a fair bargain. As a man of bargains and business, her father must admit its equity.

Ten days later Alton Pennoyer, Valentine, and Max Welton, an engineer who had already put in a summer at Farewell on the payroll of the Irrigation Company, started westward.

Father and daughter were scarcely settled in the latter's drawing room when the Pullman conductor appeared with a telegram. After glancing at the typewritten sheet, Pennoyer handed it to Valentine who read:

"Have assurances favorable action if local public opinion not hostile. If you approve intend to arrange issue special edition newspaper here boosting project. This will cinch matter. Heartily recommend it. Can buy paper outright later if desired and so control situation. Wire.
"FAILING."

"Which means?" she asked.

"That Failing is no fool. And my dear, if we pull this off I don't anticipate much further trouble —not even from your devoted admirer!" He smiled grimly. "As a prospective son-in-law (his own prospecting, of course) it strikes me that young man of yours is a good deal of an ass."

"What did you say?" Valentine inquired when her father had finished his reply to the telegram.

"Just this: 'I approve your plan.'" Then, with mock seriousness he added, "Do you?"

"Yes . . . if it works!" and they both smiled, each foreseeing the successful culmination of a different scheme.

Arrival Unexpected 149

During the next four days Valentine had ample time to analyze her plans and herself (a favorite occupation, never very productive) while she saw from her window the shores of Lake Michigan, the everlasting agricultural reaches of the continental midregions, the sagebrush semi-deserts and "bad lands" of the intermountain country, and, finally, the magnificent Columbia.

To Valentine the trip was tiresome, and the end of it dusty, dirty, and quite lacking the inspiration she had expected. However, Welton was attentive and amusing. He talked well and never seemed travel stained. Before they crossed the Missouri she had dubbed him "The Life Saver," a title won by persistent good humor and constant efforts to make the journey as pleasant as possible. Despite the leavening of his presence, however, she was nearly sick of her bargain after the dirty journey from the Columbia south to Shaniko. And at Shaniko everything went wrong.

"A message for you," said the clerk at the Columbia Southern Hotel, handing Mr. Pennoyer an envelope. "It came in by telephone this morning."

The communication was from Failing, stating that as the company auto was out of commission with no substitute available he had arranged for a special stage to bring the travelers from Shaniko to Farewell. They were to commence the one-hundred-mile drive at daybreak. With a light rig and frequent changes of horses they should reach Farewell by dark.

That night was a miserable one for the Pennoyers. The hotel's best rooms were directly over the bar, and the bar was prosperously noisy. It was midnight before Valentine dropped into a fitful sleep. Almost immediately, it seemed to her, someone pounded on her door.

"Five o'clock!"

The mirror was cracked, the water in the thick white pitcher was icy cold. The room smelt musty, out-of-doors looked tragically cold and gray, and her feelings corresponded with the environment. Worse than that, she seemed unable to appear other than she felt, which made her furious. She was sick of it all. Oregon she hated. Everything connected with the trip she detested. Anyone who enthused over such a country she pitied.

By the time the stage rattled beneath the juniper trees on the outskirts of Farewell, she was utterly at the end of her tether. Never had she been so weary, so uncomfortable, and so bedraggled. And withal she was bitterly resentful because she felt at her worst when she craved to look her best.

Yet when the stage halted in front of Farewell Inn and the cloud of dust had dissipated Valentine felt curiously disappointed. David was not there to greet her!

To be sure, so far as she was concerned Kent had no reason to believe her nearer than Manhattan Island, and ten minutes previously she had

Arrival Unexpected 151

thought herself unwilling to meet him. But all that made no difference just then. After a hundred miles of eating dust she had no appetite for logic. The fact of the minute was that David had failed her.

Scarcely had Alton Pennoyer and his daughter been assisted from the vehicle when behind them sounded the strangest voice Valentine had ever heard. It started with an impressive boom, and then abruptly jumped six notes to a vocal altitude ridiculously unmasculine.

"How *do* you do! Mr. Pennoyer—ah, Mr. Welton—glad to see you. Enchanted, I'm sure, Miss Pennoyer . . . this is indeed an honor for Farewell."

As Failing was explaining the difficulties with the automobile, the sound of running footsteps clattering along the wooden sidewalk caused the little group to turn.

"David!" cried Valentine. And then, as he came nearer, "My goodness! Why, you're . . ." but whatever she intended to say was left unsaid.

Disregarding the others, David Kent went straight up to Valentine and clasping her two hands looked full in her face. It was a searching look, questioning . . . and then all at once radiant.

Nor was the girl's sudden silence and the young man's frank adoration lost upon the others. Failing, astonished at the unexpected development, showed his perplexity. Welton, who up to then had heard little of Kent, smirked outwardly and boiled inwardly. Alton Pennoyer positively snorted.

Rarely did Valentine Pennoyer lose command of a situation, and her poise, routed temporarily, speedily returned to her.

She withdrew her hands from Kent's.

"Yes, you've changed . . . no doubt of that," her tone was back at normal. She strove to be super-commonplace.

"Have I?" Kent could not draw his eyes away. "For the better?" he inquired eagerly.

She laughed, and there was a passing hint of bitterness in the laughter. All at once Valentine recalled how weary she was and how poorly her beauty was prepared for such a meeting by the dust and dirt of the long ride, her soiled and wrinkled clothing, and her lack of rest. It annoyed her. It seemed unfair . . . and on top of that here was Kent attempting to monopolize her, almost to assert proprietary rights.

"No . . . not for the better." Her patrician head was held high as she appraised him. "You're brown, but I suppose one has to be either that or dirty in this wretched country. Then you look older. And as for clothes" . . . she smiled a trifle cynically . . . "if you want to know, I think they're positively dreadful. You look like . . . why, at home you'd actually pass for a *rowdy!*"

"Oh, thank you, thank you!" Kent mocked good-naturedly, but the sunniness left his face.

Dapper Welton, catching the note of sarcasm, beamed.

"*Ahem!*" boomed Alton Pennoyer in a preparatory way. It was high time to break up this ridiculous tête-à-tête.

"Glad to see you, Kent," said the financier dryly, stepping forward and taking the young man's hand.

"Thanks. I hope you are!"

"This is Mr. Welton . . . Max, Mr. Kent . . . an old friend of . . ." it was on the tip of his tongue to say "Valentine's" but instead he substituted "of the family."

"How are you?" Welton put the routine greeting disinterestedly.

Something in the natty appearance of the engineer annoyed Kent inexplicably. It was a case of no love at first sight.

"Oh, I'm pretty *rowdyish*, thanks."

Kent grinned. Welton looked surprised, Valentine annoyed.

"What next, Failing?" inquired Pennoyer, indicating the luggage. "Oh, I beg pardon . . . of course you know our friend here?" his gesture embraced Kent.

Failing's countenance bespoke the bubbling enthusiasm of a professional mourner.

"I have had . . . that pleasure." The manager rubbed together his beefy hands, the wrinkles deepening about his eyes in what was intended to be a smile.

As they walked to the Company House, Valentine chatted with Kent who carried her bags.

"Mr. Failing doesn't exactly love you, does he?"

"Not exactly."

His apparent preoccupation annoyed her.

"You're not very enthusiastic," she pouted.

"About what?"

"Me!"

"*Good Lord.*" That was all he said for a space. Then seriously: "You're changed too, Val . . . or perhaps it's just I."

"Do I look badly?" Her words followed her thoughts. Instinctively she coiled back a vagrant lock of hair.

"*Badly?*" He looked at her then, from the disheveled dark hair framing her refined face to the tips of her well clad feet, and his eyes saw nothing that did not seem perfection. "*Badly?*" he echoed, and surely the wonder in the word and the expression of the speaker's face must have gratified the eternal feminine thirst for homage. After a long second of silence Kent continued, as if it were difficult to find adequate words to convey his thoughts. "Val, see that mountain . . . so white and wonderfully, perfectly beautiful?"

They were on the green lawn before the Company House, almost at the very edge of Welcome River. Across the water, which was blue with the reflection of the sky, there were fine straight pine trees, and thirty miles beyond rose the Chief. With the dark pines before it and the blue sky behind it, the great white mountain did indeed seem perfection.

"It is attractive, David."

"Attractive? Why, to me that's the most beautiful view in the world . . . the most absolutely perfect thing . . . except *one*." Turning from the beautiful mountain to the beautiful girl, he looked full at her. He had a queer trick of unexpected seriousness.

"Now," said he, "I am looking at something more perfect even than my mountain."

She blushed at this pretty answer to her question, dropping him a mock courtesy to hide it.

"And perhaps" . . . he followed his train of thought to its ending, speaking half to himself . . . "perhaps it's equally unattainable."

"What did you say? I didn't hear." The low words had escaped her. He laughed shortly.

"It's a long way to the mountain as the trail goes . . ."

"Very cold, that mountain country!" Max Welton interrupted, just then coming up behind them.

Turning to the engineer she expressed her agreement with a smiling nod. "It does look so. You know, Mr. Welton, I don't believe I'd like mountains . . . except at a distance."

CHAPTER XVI

ACCIDENT UNFORTUNATE

On the afternoon following her arrival, Kent and Valentine walked leisurely to the base of the Pilot, chatting on the way of trivial things and safely far-away people.

"Can you make it?" He indicated the climb.

"Good gracious!" Valentine looked up at the butte and down at her feet. "I'm not keen on mountain climbing," she demurred.

"When in Rome . . ." he laughed.

"I don't believe the best families on the Forum climbed the Seven Hills."

"Well, we haven't any best families out here . . . thank Heaven."

"David—you sound like a Hull House lecturer or an anarchist . . . or something. And besides" . . . she added more seriously . . . "you talk about 'we' as if you belonged here—which of course you don't."

"No, I suppose I don't belong, Val," he replied dryly. "But it's hard not to get the habit out here of talking about 'our' country and 'our' town—and boasting about it, too. You see, in the West everyone is wonderfully proud of everything from its grain to its" ... he was going to say "girls" but substituted . . . "to its gophers. It's local patriotism in the *n'th* degree."

"Or conceit?" Valentine interposed disinterestedly. She was bored enough with the West and its ways without having Kent discourse upon them.

He laughed.

"Perhaps . . . and I'm getting as bad as the rest. You didn't like my old Roman adage, so how's this? When in Paris be a parasite . . . and I'll feel like one if we don't get a move on."

A third of the way up the butte Valentine awoke to the realization that it was about three times higher, and harder to negotiate than she had anticipated. With two thirds of the stony trail behind, she was ready to quit. But encouraged by Kent's reassurances that the sunset view from the top was worth all the effort, and even more effectively aided by his willing arm, the girl scrambled with increasing weariness up the steep trail, thoroughly uncomfortable and rapidly becoming as short of patience as she was of breath.

"Are those animal tracks, David?" she inquired during a brief halt, pointing to lines which wound, corkscrewlike, around and up the side of the butte. While actually formed by water draining down the soft slopes they curiously resembled trails.

He nodded gravely.

"But surely there aren't any wild beasts so

near town?" There was a note of alarm in her voice.

"Don't worry, Val . . . they're not really dangerous. Their scientific name is *sambucus pubens* but hereabout they're called *lava hops*. In such cases I always prefer the local no-men-cla-ture!" Here a severe fit of coughing seized the elucidating scientist; so severe, in fact, that he was obliged to turn his back to Valentine.

"They're certainly queer beasts," Kent continued, his eyes intent on the western sky line. "Notice how all the trails—paths, you know—curve around to the right as they climb upward? That's because the lava hops have their right legs longer than their left ones. Curious provision of thoughtful old mother nature, that." . . . Again a short spasm of coughing interrupted him. . . . "You see, by always working around to the right as they climb, their right legs being longer, it keeps their bodies level no matter how steep the hill. And of course when they get on flat ground the difference in the length of their legs gives them a sort of hopping gait, and from that and the fact that they are found only in this lava country they get their name 'lava hop.'"

It was Valentine's first intimate encounter with the wonders of western natural history. What a capital story to take home for retelling at dinners next season! If she only actually could see one!

"As to their looks" . . . Kent answered her query . . . "why, they're a bit like a cougar when it comes to their hide," . . . she shivered . . . "but not ferocious . . . not *very* that is. They're larger than a badger and a bit smaller than the average black bear. Why" . . . he leaned over a bit of dust beside them . . . "a lava hop's been right here!"

Sure enough, an animal's track showed in the brown dirt.

"It looks a little like a dog," Valentine offered sagely.

"Yes, so it does. But notice this hind pad"— with his finger he indicated a part of the track. "*There* is where the difference comes. But let's get on to the top. Perhaps on the way down we'll meet a *sambucus pubens* face to face . . . they usually come out after sundown."

The Pilot was the show spot, and the showing spot, of Farewell. An obliging providence had placed it as an observation tower whence all the details of the surrounding country might be viewed. Visitors were dragged to its summit to become acquainted with the topography of the region. Timber buyers spied out the lie of the land from its convenient top, determining just where the forests sloped most advantageously to mill sites on the river, and then going forth and buying their timber claims from the settlers for about a third of their ultimate market value. And tight-mouthed railroad engineers, quietly reconnoitering, had spent many an hour on the Pilot studying the far-reaching railroadless land which lay stretched in a nature-made map at their feet, and later silently slipping away in the guise of timber cruisers, stock buyers, or land seekers.

Finally they reached the summit and rested on the western lip of the old crater, with Farewell and a goodly portion of Central Oregon spread out before them, while Kent talked of the various landmarks and told incidents of the country's brief history. West and south from the town, whose scattered roofs they glimpsed among the trees where Welcome River wound like a silver band, the pine lands billowed up from the level country and over the foothills to the white peaks of the mountain range.

Away from the mountains he showed her the huge plain stretching like a flat gray table for forty miles, and tilted a bit to the east and north, quite perfectly planned for irrigation. To the east, near the Pilot, were many square patches of green, checkerboarding dun squares. The green, he told her, were alfalfa fields, and the dun sagebrush comprised the others, where irrigation had as yet left the land unleavened. The canals and laterals showed like thin white threads winding here and there across the country.

"That is just the beginning," declared Kent. "Beyond that ridge to the southeast there's a country as big as Massachusetts, and to-day there aren't more than five hundred people in it and I don't suppose that many acres of cultivated soil. Nothing but jackrabbits, cattle, and fuzztails."

"Fuzztails?" she repeated.

"That's what they call the range horses—scrubby little cayuses hard enough to thrive on a barbed wire diet. And Val," . . . his enthusiasm carried him on, . . . "don't you see what all this means? It's the story of the frontier all over again. The big chances have not gone. There's a million acres over there beyond Cow Ridge, most of it wheat land as good as the Palouse country."

But there was no answering chord of enthusiasm in the girl. From Cow Ridge behind which, her companion declared, lay an untouched El Dorado, her eyes returned to the little patches of irrigated land and the larger areas of brown waste untouched by water.

"David," she sighed whimsically, "I'm afraid you've been bitten by this western booster bug. Don't you think you ought to get away before you're inoculated?"

"What do *you* want me to do?" He put the question in a low, serious tone, looking straight at her.

"Well," she parried, "what do you want to do yourself?"

"I . . . don't know." He was silent for a minute. "Yes; I do know . . . one thing . . . the only important thing, Val dear . . . I want to marry you!"

She laughed lightly.

"But that's nothing new!"

She thought him very handsome as he bent over

her, despite the shabby clothes—so brown and strong. Bending still further, suddenly he took the beautiful face in his two hands and pressed his mouth to her red lips in a fiery kiss, crushing her to him for a passionate moment.

She had been silent, unresisting. Then, as he drew back, indignation surged within her, yet, somehow, subtly tempered with satisfaction. But dominating her tangled emotions was amazement at the impetuous abandon of her lover. Could this surprising man be the same David Kent—that patient, trustworthy, always safe David, whose placid nature she had toyed with so often?

"David!" Her heart suddenly harbored genuine apprehension. For her transgressed lips somehow failed to utter the words of reproach she knew they should, and her cool blood for once raced hotly through her body.

It was Kent who controlled himself first.

"I'm sorry, Val," he said, simply. "Just couldn't help it." He was still half drunk with desire to embrace her, and to evade the temptation drew his eyes from the lovely girl, who in her agitation appeared doubly alluring. "I guess it must be the air out here. I used to be able to behave myself."

His back was toward her now and her eyes were upon him. Had he turned just then something in those misty gray-blue eyes might have told him that there are times when behaving one's self need not be the ultimate goal of manly ambition.

"Perhaps," she ventured, and her voice faltered wistfully, "perhaps it's your clothes . . . *Mr. Rowdy!*"

"You'll forgive me?"

"No!" The warning note in her voice checked his advance. "No . . . I'm not angry . . . not *very*, that is! . . . only you mustn't ever do it again. You see," she went on, with regained steadiness, "it's not only . . . well, let's say *unseemly*, but it's also breaking your contract—the rules of the game."

"I only promised not to ask you to marry me until . . . let's see . . . until next May. That's when the year is up."

She laughed.

"And what do you call your recent actions?"

"Oh, that was simply . . . well, showing my appreciation for the beauties of nature!"

"Don't do it again, David, that's all." She was serious. "And before we go I want some information."

"Oh Lord!" said Kent to himself. "Here comes trouble."

"David, who is the man fighting my father?"

"I believe his name is . . . Kent." He looked at her gravely. "That is, Val, I understand he has been making a little trouble, and is in a fair way to make more."

"You didn't come here to meddle in other people's business."

She was on her own ground now. Her intense

loyalty to her father and her belief in the absolute right of all that concerned him was in a way even more fundamental than her own personal selfishness. So it was small wonder that Kent's lengthy explanation of the situation had slight effect.

He told the girl what had happened to the water users and what was destined to overtake them. From where they stood the brown level lands of the South Canal segregation were visible, and he explained how the profits of this new unit were sought by the company while at the same time it ignored the rights and almost the very existence of the original settlers who had bought land and were waiting for water.

"Well, why shouldn't they sell this new land?" she asked when she had heard him through. "You say yourself the profits would be enough to fix up the old ditches and all the rest of it."

The chief reason why the extra acreage should not be sold, as Kent was aware, was the lack of sufficient water in Welcome River to care for the new as well as the original segregation. But he doubted whether Alton Pennoyer knew that his engineer's report on the river's flow was crooked, and that sufficient water actually did not exist. So he attempted no answer to her question.

"Dads is going to be positively wild." Valentine herself cared little for the paternal anger, being always able to circumvent it, but when directed at others she had the highest respect for its devastating efficiency.

Kent nodded. "My friend Failing will help that along."

"But it would be very easy to put him under obligation to you. And I think" . . . she continued, regarding him keenly . . . "*that* would help . . . in other directions."

"I've considered that," he said, almost sharply. "In fact, that's about all I have thought about since yesterday when I found out who was behind this blamed irrigating company . . ."

"Yesterday? You only knew it yesterday?" She was genuinely surprised, and still more so when he told her the circumstances of his double discovery of her father's interest in the B. I. C. and her own coming.

"You'd have me quit? Val, I thought you wanted me to make good . . . to stick to something until I finished it and came out on top."

"But where are you getting?"

"Only into trouble, I suppose," he said bitterly.

Valentine was annoyed. She had expected to find Kent reasonably ready to fall in with her suggestion to quit Farewell and its vexatious settlers, especially if by so doing he should win the favor of her father. And instead of jumping at the chance, he inclined to platitudes about making good.

"It is time we started back," she declared. The sun was already enveloped behind the purple outlines of the Chief, and the long shadows of the range suddenly engulfed them.

Before they reached the bottom of the butte the dusk had thickened into near-darkness. But disregarding the difficulties of picking their way, and because it was really easier to go fast than slow, they raced down the final pitch of the descent in regular schoolboy fashion. And just at the end of it the girl's feet tripped over a stone, throwing her headlong down the steep slope.

She lay so quiet he thought she had fainted. But Valentine was simply fighting for self control. Pride kept her from whimpering, or from speaking until she was sure of herself.

"Ouch! It's my ankle, David." She twisted in pain. "I turned it on that stone . . . oh! but it hurts."

Kent started to unlace her shoe, and finding the handling too painful, slashed it asunder with his knife. Further than releasing the foot and resting it as comfortably as possible, there seemed nothing he could do as no water was available. So he placed the sweater he had been carrying under and around the girl's shoulders, stripped off his flannel shirt and wrapped the swelling ankle in it, as warmly and restfully as possible.

"I hate to leave you alone, but it won't take me over half an hour to get a rig, Val," he said gently, after a moment's thought. "I'll run all the way in."

Until he spoke she had considered nothing but the pain of the minute.

"You're not going to leave me?" There was terror in her voice.

"Yes, Val." He tightened his belt. "It's the only thing to do. We might wait here all night without a soul coming this way. And the longer I keep you from a doctor the worse the ankle will get."

"Oh!" said she, and that was all.

"I'm terribly sorry . . ." which indeed he was. "Try to be cheerful . . . good-by!"

With that he was off, in an orderly dog trot, intent upon conserving his energy so as to cover the long mile to Farewell as speedily as possible.

"*Oh!*" said the girl again, and this time the word ended in a sob. She looked around at the gathering darkness, a little wildly, and up at the sides of the butte marked with the strange corkscrew trails.

"*Cheerful!*" By now she was crying outright. She wished for David at her side—for some protector—above everything else. And David was pounding along the dusty road to town.

CHAPTER XVII

FIRST AID

"IF you tell, it will ruin me." The tone was masculine and resentful.

"If I don't it may ruin hundreds." It was a woman's voice, pitched low and infinitely troubled.

"But I did it under orders." The man's voice sounded querulous. "Loyalty is a first rule of business . . . anyone knows that."

"How about loyalty to one's self?"

"Don't preach please." He was curt now. "That's all pretty enough in story books. There's highbrow ethics, and business ethics . . . they generally don't mix worth a cent."

"Did someone tell you to fake those records?" There was a quiver of hope in the words.

The answer was a growl and an oath. They were quite near now, and Valentine could hear the light lava gravel crunch beneath the man's shoes as he turned upon his companion.

"I don't care who did it or how it was done!" he snarled, and to the listening girl the voice sounded oddly familiar. "I stand by my guns—

and by the Old Man. As for you, young lady, my advice is to keep your precious mouth shut."

In the black silence following the outbreak the unsuspected member of the triangle thought she heard a sob, quickly stifled.

"It was all a mistake between us two," the man's voice was gentler. "Plain folly, that's what it was . . . just like my telling you about the report. It's ended now . . . absolutely ended. That's best for both of us . . . we're awake after a fool dream. I'm glad . . . damn glad! Well, I'm off to town. Yes, I know you don't mind the dark. Good-by . . . and remember!"

For a moment Valentine thought she was deserted again, and would have called as the man's footfalls receded, but all at once the half choking sound of sobs that would not be denied was close at hand. She tried to turn on her side, then to see something, if possible, of the companion fate seemed to have guided to her. The movement brought a distressing throb in her ankle.

"Ouch!" she cried as the hot pain shot through it.

"Oh! What's that?" The other one was startled now.

"It's me!" called Valentine, with neither logic nor grammar.

Then the other woman took shape among the night shadows and, coming to Valentine, tended her with efficient gentleness, the while asking her the how and the why of her situation.

Briefly Valentine answered that she had sprained her ankle racing down the butte and that her companion had left her there while he went to town for aid.

"Who did you say it was? I wonder if he knows where to get a physician and a rig."

"Mr. Kent."

"Oh."

"Do you know him?"

"Yes, I know him." The other girl said it quite colorlessly, yet something in her tone—perhaps in its very evenness—piqued Valentine.

"Do you suppose he has enough intelligence to get me out of this fix he got me into?" she asked.

Instead of answering, the other knelt down, and in a few seconds a tiny blaze of twigs and branches of the oily sagebrush sprang up from beneath her hands. As she turned from the kindling fire, Valentine for the first time saw the open strong face of this one whom chance had sent through the night to her side.

"Perhaps that will make it a little warmer, Miss Pennoyer." The fair-haired girl smiled pleasantly.

"How do you know my name?"

"I didn't—but I guessed it. Most everyone knows that Alton Pennoyer and his daughter are 'in these parts.'"

"And yours?"

"Crete Colton."

Then a short silence. The fire warmed Valentine, its glow and the companionship cheered her, and for the moment her ankle was less troublesome.

"I suppose you and Mr. . . . er, that is, David, have often climbed the Pilot?" The eastern girl tried to say it casually.

"No, not often." Crete looked full at Valentine, smiling frankly. "Only twice, I think. You see" . . . she wanted to set at rest then and there further misunderstanding . . . "Mr. Kent has been a good deal at the Jones place, where I stay, so naturally we've taken a few tramps together."

Crete was at the point of diplomatically adding that the young man was to her mind extremely dull company because his thoughts always seemed far away, when that perennial defamer of the calm of western nights, the coyote, lifted afar his plaintive voice. At the sudden sound all the terrors of her forsaken loneliness returned to Valentine. She had never heard a coyote howl, and lying there in the sagebrush, with the black night around, the uncanny wail chilled her marrow.

"Oh!" she cried, "what's that?" And then, as silence settled down again, "Was it a lava hop? Is there any danger?"

"We're as safe as at home—only a coyote." Crete's calmness amazed Valentine. Evidently this girl who wandered casually about in the night cared nothing at all for marauding brutes . . . queer indeed were these feminine products of the West! "But," continued Crete, "what was that animal you mentioned?"

"A lava hop . . . one of those queer beasts which make the paths on the side of the butte."

"Oh," said Crete.

"Yes," Valentine continued seriously, "naturally I thought it was one of them. Before you came I was scared to death thinking what I'd do if a lava hop attacked me. You see, of course I was quite helpless . . . but David said they're usually not dangerous."

"No, not usually."

Crete laughed, and her mirth was boyish and hearty.

"Well?" Valentine was annoyed.

"Who told you about the lava hops?"

"David."

Crete laughed again. Then all at once the truth dawned upon Valentine. But instead of causing her to smile, comprehension of the little hoax kindled her to anger, very suddenly and very hotly. Miss Valentine Pennoyer had been made a laughing stock and before a frowzy-haired western wench, at that! And David had done it! She bit her lip.

"Oh, that's nothing," chuckled Crete. "Tenderfeet are always getting little games put up on them. Why, when David first came he put in a solid day fishing on Lone Butte canal when everyone here knows there's a fish screen at the intake and not a solitary trout in the whole ditch. That's regular. The lava hop yarn, however," . . . she smiled again, . . . "is newer and more polished

... it really took an ex-tenderfoot to concoct that, and a real one to swallow it!"

Whereat Miss Pennoyer was still more annoyed. To have David Kent play silly tricks upon her was bad enough, but to be called a tenderfoot by a country girl was worse.

So Crete was still chuckling and Valentine was fuming increasingly when the sound of horses' hoofs and the distant twinkle of a lantern announced the arrival of the malefactor himself.

"You're all right now," Crete said. "I think I'll go." Suiting the action to the word, she disappeared in the darkness.

The team drew up.

"Hallo, Val," called Kent cheerily. "A fire, eh? That's cozy!"

The very word put Valentine on edge. Cozy! To be deserted for an hour, left lying on the ground in the dark, half perishing from cold and with a sprained ankle—save the mark if that was coziness!

"I couldn't find the doctor but I got someone just as good—or a bit better." Kent was down from the wagon with a jump, and beside him the girl saw a stocky figure. "Valentine, you remember Bishop Rudd?"

She recalled the Bishop clearly. In fact, the recollection which struck her just then was her mother's account of having once spanked this same Bishop when he was a boy, and a bad boy at that. The memory struck her as so absurd she commenced laughing, and then all at once the laughter became hysterical and turned to weeping as the reaction of the experience set in.

"I wanted a *doctor!*" she sobbed.

"But I just couldn't get a doctor," Kent interposed gently. "The only one in Farewell was out on a case. However, Val," he added reassuringly, "the Bishop really knows a lot about first-aid work and can handle that ankle just as well as any sawbones."

Something in the efficient and silent way in which Bishop Rudd went about his task evidently reassured Valentine, for in a few minutes she regained self-control and lay quiet as the amateur physician bathed the injured ankle with cool water from the desert water bag and then wrapped it securely with a gauze bandage.

In the meanwhile Kent replenished the fire so as to have more light for the Bishop's activities.

"By the way, Val, who made this fire?" It suddenly struck him that Valentine of course could not have done it herself.

"Eh, what's that?" The Bishop looked up from his work.

"Why, when I left there wasn't any fire here. I asked who made it."

Valentine lay very still now, with her eyes shut. For perhaps half a minute she did not reply.

"If it hadn't been for the fire I suppose the lava hops might have attacked me?" The girl spoke acidly, her eyes still closed.

"Lava hops?" echoed the Bishop inquiringly.

"Ask Mr. Kent."

"Good Lord, Val, I forgot all about that . . . that little yarn," he looked down at her as some measure of comprehension stole over him. "Why, you poor little girl! You don't mean to say you lay there worrying about those fool beasts?"

"Only for a time." Her voice was colder even than she herself had been. "No . . . please don't do that" . . . he had knelt and started to slip his arm beneath her head . . . "it was only a little while before I learned you had been lying . . . a friend of yours told me."

"Who?"

"Who climbed the butte with you last?" Her eyes were open now.

Kent thought a minute.

"Why, I guess it was Crete Colton."

"Exactly!"

"And she built the fire?"

Valentine nodded.

"Where is she now?" Kent looked around.

"I don't know . . . and don't care. If you want" . . . the color was mounting into Valentine's cheeks . . . "go find her!"

CHAPTER XVIII

A CASUAL QUESTION

OCTOBER ripened with sunny splendor at Farewell, intoxicatingly bright and crisply clear, the hazes of summer all washed away by the first autumn rains. Distance, measured by the eye, dwindled into nothingness.

For ten days her sprained ankle kept Valentine a prisoner at the Company House, much of the time ensconced on the porch, and waited on by her limited court, comprising Kent, Welton, Rudd, and Failing.

The ideal weather availed Valentine not at all. Indeed her inability to utilize its out-of-door invitations no whit abated her fretful discontent. Fundamentally she knew nothing of, and cared less for, such recreation as the Oregon hills, forests, and streams offered; but now that she was there, to be prevented from even sampling these offerings tormented her. And the more Kent, sitting at her feet, told of the Open, the more rebellious she became.

"You're positively talking me sick about this country . . . I'm getting to hate it," she would burst forth when Kent enthused too wantonly.

And her suitor would laugh and try to take her hand in his, often with temporary success.

"Next year," he would continue gayly, "I will initiate you. See the old Chief? Well, there's the most beautifulest camp site the Lord ever created, just below that long snow slide . . . practically perfect for a honeymoon camp. Once you've had a real taste of the mountains you'll be wild about it."

Valentine then would say little or nothing, in her heart convinced her lover was absurdly unreasonable. And after he left she would try to analyze this western madness which had overcome him, considering how best to let him know, once and for all, that she entertained no remote notion of adopting Farewell and its out-of-doors for her own, nor even, for that matter, of accepting the most alluring honeymoon invitations . . . unless with very different environment.

"Well, Val dear," Alton Pennoyer declared one noon, after a morning with Failing at the office, "everything is rounding up nicely now. The Land Board seems ready to stand for the new unit, if there's no strong objection up here. They've got political jobs, you know, and keep their ears to the ground for the growls of the dear electorate."

Valentine, in the hammock on the porch, smiled up at her father. It was refreshing to find him in a cheerful mood for once, for the squabbles of the irrigationists had kept him well on edge.

"There won't be any growls, then, Dads?"

"No. That is" . . . the speaker smiled as he stroked his crisp mustache . . . "there won't be any you can hear down at Salem."

She asked him about Failing's plan for a special edition of the *Pioneer*, of which he had wired when they left New York.

"That's all fixed. Just went over the last article. Old Pharaoh Jones, the editor, begins setting the type this afternoon. It will be shipped to me at Portland . . ."

"Then you're going to Portland? Oh! Dads . . ."

"I have to, Val. But it will only be for a few days and you'll be quite comfortable here. Failing is going to the hotel so you'll have the place to yourself. And by the way, wouldn't it be a good idea to get some woman to stay with you?"

Valentine considered the proposition for a minute. Then an idea struck her.

"Yes, that would be best. I'll ask Miss Colton."

"Miss Colton?" The name meant nothing to Pennoyer.

"She's a girl I met the other day."

"All right. Better get her promptly as I'm leaving to-morrow."

Shortly after lunch, when her father and Failing had appropriated to themselves the big "main room" of the Company House with their heads together over maps and papers, Valentine, upon the porch, spied Bishop Rudd. Answering her call he came across the grass, thick chested, tanned, and clear of eye, with the ever-present smile hovering about his generous mouth.

"A regular old-fashioned girl!" he greeted her. "On the piazza . . . in a hammock and . . . no, I see it's not embroidery but a novel, which fills the bill quite as well." He seated himself on the top step, where the sunshine enveloped him and his own sunny smile enveloped her. "You know, I'm afraid I'm a reactionary—the old-fashioned dainty hammock girl makes such a hit with me!"

She was genuinely pleased with the compliment, which had the ring of sincerity. But after all why shouldn't he compliment her? Didn't she look adorably attractive in her negligee creation of chiffon and crêpe de chine of palest green? Her own glance, on a roving commission of self appraisement, even took stock of the shapely member which extended alluringly just over the edge of the hammock displaying an abbreviated expanse of silken ankle, while its bandaged and unsightly mate was banished from observation beneath a gayly oriental shawl.

"But I'm not old fashioned!" she objected.

"You don't look *old*, of course . . . but please don't deny looking old fashioned. Really, it's most becoming."

"Bishop, which do *you* like better?" The girl's voice was half joking, half earnest. "The hammock girl or the other kind . . . the out door well-I-should-say-I-can-take-care-of-myself variety?"

The Bishop laughed outright.

"I suppose I mean the so-called typical western girl," Valentine added.

"I don't go much on types, myself," he replied. "You see, to my mind, there's no such thing to-day as a 'typical' western woman or man, any more than there is a 'typical' American. We're all composite photographs printed from countless exposures but developed each in an individual solution."

"Anyway, you'll admit the girls of the West aren't . . . well, the 'old-fashioned' kind you were enthusing over just now?"

The Bishop was thoughtful for a moment.

"I see just what you mean," he said, "and it's true enough out here the woods are full of the competent, take-care-of-herself kind, as you put it. And do you know, when I consider the problem" . . . he paused, pressing his lips together in a quizzical way he had, while his eyes twinkled . . . "I'm totally unable to make a decision . . . I'm neutral. However, my ideal would be a combination of the two. . . ."

"A harem?"

"Hardly! Say the graces of the drawing-room combined with the attributes of the open. I suppose though," . . . he heaved a heavy mock sigh, . . . "such perfection exists only in the dreams of an ageing ecclesiastical bachelor."

Valentine liked this plain, outspoken churchman almost despite herself. His singular, blunt informality contrasted oddly with the graces and mental furbelows of the squires of the cloth with whom she had sipped tea in transcontinental drawing-rooms.

"What is Mr. Kent's ideal?" She asked it lightly, and then tucked back a disorderly lock spied in the tiny mirror that dangled from a slight golden chain around her neck.

The little Bishop got up from the step, and when he had his stocky legs firmly beneath his thick strong body he stood for a moment silently until she looked up at him.

"I think," said the little Bishop meeting her eyes earnestly, "that the easiest way for you to see David Kent's ideal . . . would be to look in your mirror again."

Valentine blushed prettily, quite consciously contented.

She changed the subject then, telling Rudd of her father's departure the following day and her desire to secure a companion to share the Company House with her.

"So . . . for contrast's sake as well as company! . . . East is East and West is West, you know . . . I want to ask Miss Colton to stay with me until Dads comes back. Won't you please act as my courier?"

He acquiesced promptly, even insisting that the formality of a written invitation was entirely unnecessary, despite Valentine's protests.

"I was going by the *Pioneer* shop anyway and I'll just drop in and tell her—she's pretty sure to be there," he said. "You see, 'jes passin' the word' is quite *comme il faut* in this neck of the woods."

"I hope the poor thing has something fit to wear . . . and that she doesn't eat with her knife!" the young lady said to herself when the Bishop had gone. Then, rearranging the pillows and with the passing thought that comparisons often are desirable in the education of masculine appreciation, she assumed the serious contemplation of her novel.

Alton Pennoyer was in the midst of a cigar and a sentence when he and Failing emerged from their conference.

Pennoyer was saying, "They must leave Shaniko Sunday morning. Express 'em direct to me so they'll be delivered first thing Monday morning."

Failing nodded.

"The Board gets in from Salem about noon. We'll have lunch and then adjourn to my sitting-room for cigars and a wee nip. The first thing you know one of 'em will see a copy of the *Pioneer* lying around casually and he'll pick it up."

"And they'll fall all over themselves!" ejaculated Failing. "Once they find out from the paper that the country is keen for the new unit there'll be nothing to it. It'll tickle 'em, too, because those follows don't want any trouble . . . just the minute they discover the plan has popular backing instead of opposition they'll have nervous prostration in their hurry to sign up the contract."

"Maybe," said Pennoyer. "At least, I hope so—and I'll admit it looks reasonable. But there'll have to be another formal meeting at Salem."

"I wouldn't delay a minute longer than absolutely necessary," Failing advised. "I know these blamed State boards—don't give them a chance to figure much or ask too many questions. They're worse than weather vanes when it comes to shifting around."

"Leave it to me!" The financier smiled complacently.

Dapper young Welton appeared just then, greeting Valentine pleasantly and his employer with a respectfulness which to the girl seemed very appropriate. With a word of cordial salutation he took the young engineer by the arm and led him into the house.

"By Gad, Miss Valentine, he's a wonder!" Failing brandished his thick thumb in the direction of the door. "*He's* got the punch and drive . . . *and* the ideas." The burly manager enthused oilily.

"Yes?" said Valentine, absentmindedly. The words conjured up some memory, which she sought to visualize. Then suddenly the conversation overheard at the foot of Lone Butte came back to her.

"Do they call Dads the 'Old Man'?" she asked.

The quick question took the manager unaware. "Why yes," he stuttered, "they do call him that sometimes. You see, most always the boss anywhere out here is called the 'old man' . . . no matter how really young he is," he added, as an afterthought, and wound up with a chuckle that was intended to be ingratiating; "it's sort of a term of . . . of endearment, you might say."

It was not Failing anyway, whom she had heard talking with Crete Colton.

However, she would try again. It was quite an amusing experiment . . . and she might stumble upon the identity of that nocturnal voice.

"Who told him to fake the records?" The question was nothing more than a whim, and she was prepared to laugh at his expected mystification.

But though mystification suffused Failing's face it was of a quality so extraordinary as to startle Valentine almost as much as her own innocent words had startled the manager.

"The records?" His voice faltered uncertainly.

"Why yes . . . who actually faked them?" The audacity of her rôle astonished Valentine herself. She felt she was playing with gunpowder, yet enjoyed the experience in a dubious fashion.

"Your father had no hand in it, Miss Pennoyer, . . . rest assured of that."

Valentine, thoroughly startled, swung around to face Crete Colton, who stood on the lawn at the edge of the porch. The western girl regarded her steadily, with a kindly smile.

"I'm sorry I overheard you," Crete continued in her quiet voice. "You didn't notice me coming across the grass—and I couldn't help hearing your question . . . I'm really glad you know about it."

"About what?"

"Why, the records."

"*What records?*" All at once Valentine felt acutely annoyed. She had capitalized that chance remark about the mysterious records more from a spirit of mischief than anything else, and now, behold, it had created a scene with the manager and elucidated something in the nature of a defense of her own father from this stranger girl.

It was Crete's turn to be puzzled, and she showed it.

"Hallo! Sounds like a movie scene looks." Max Welton emerged from the house just in time to catch the last words. "'The fatal records, or who stole the will,' eh?" He saw only Valentine and Failing, Crete being hidden from his viewpoint. "If you want any information, Miss Pennoyer, ask me . . . I'm a regular archive when it comes to records, good, bad, and indifferent, and my motto is satisfaction guaranteed or your . . ."

The happy-go-lucky garrulity ended abruptly as

the speaker, stepping out on the porch, spied Crete.

"Yes, by all means ask him."

Crete Colton said it very evenly.

CHAPTER XIX

KING DAVID'S QUEEN

"I BEAR a royal summons," said Bishop Rudd, bowing profoundly.

"Is it to church?" She smiled. As a matter of fact she always did go on those welcome occasions when the Bishop visited Farewell.

"Nothing half so tedious. You're nominated as lady-in-waiting to the Queen."

"Queen?" Crete was puzzled. "What queen?"

"King David's queen."

"Oh!" Without enthusiasm.

So the Bishop delivered his message, adding that he thought it would be a specially nice thing to accept it.

"Perhaps. But personally I don't believe in royalty . . . it's undemocratic and strictly taboo under the Oregon system, you know. And Bishop, wasn't the Queen of Sheba . . . well, wasn't she a rather unreliable person?"

But Bishop Rudd refused to carry the discussion into the realms of biblical history, and again urging her to go to the Company House forthwith and accept for herself, went his own way.

Walking over the soft turf, the while considering whether or not she cared to accept the hospitality of the girl whom she had first seen a few nights previously beside a sagebrush fire at the base of the Pilot, Crete rounded a corner of the log house. And just as she emerged Valentine put her open sesame question about the records of the flow of Welcome River.

"Failing . . . you, too, Welton . . . come in for a minute." Pennoyer, in the doorway, beckoned his henchmen. Then he turned and went inside, having scarcely seen Crete and without noticing at all the tenseness of the four there upon the porch.

Outside the two young women faced each other.

"Too bad to interrupt the novel!" It was Crete who regained her poise first.

Valentine felt angry and mystified, in about equal proportions. The latter feeling provoked the former. She was not accustomed to mysteries and one involving her own interests, as this one somehow seemed to do, especially piqued her.

"Oh, one doesn't have to read novels here to get all the sensations of up-to-date romance," she laughed, with simulated good nature. "You people seem intent upon staging some kind of a mystery play, but for the life of me I can't tell whether it's comedy or tragedy!"

"Perhaps farce," suggested Crete, sitting on the edge of the porch with her back to a post.

"But *they*" . . . Valentine nodded toward the door just closed upon the two men . . . "they don't seem to register undiluted mirth. But to be serious . . ." She closed her book briskly. "I hope Bishop Rudd gave you my invitation, and I hope you'll accept it."

"Yes. He did . . . and I will, with pleasure."

"That's splendid. Really, I'd perish of loneliness if you wouldn't come. And there's so much I want you to tell me."

"And so much I don't intend to tell!" said Crete to herself.

The next morning, after seeing her father embarked in an automobile for Shaniko, she hobbled back to the hammock, forseeing as the most entertaining rift in the dull hours before her Crete's arrival later in the day. But another visitor came first. It was David Kent.

Even when they were spotlessly new Valentine disliked corduroys and flannel shirts, and once they acquired comparative antiquity, as had Kent's, she more than ever disapproved. His corduroys were scandalously ink stained. His flannel shirt was torn and open at the throat because there were no buttons to keep it closed, while one sleeve was rolled up to the elbow and the other ended raggedly midway between elbow and wrist. A decisive smudge of black, evidently more ink, cross-sectioned the tanned forearm, and a lesser smudge of the same brew adorned the young man's brow at the base of his towsled locks.

"Heavens! What have we now . . . a tramp, street cleaner, or simply a printer's devil?"

"A devil of a mess, I'll admit," he answered ruefully.

"Did you fall in the ink this time? Or did your editor friend have you clean the inside of the stove?"

"Neither. I simply played nursemaid to the press and changed its rollers. You see, I was feeding it . . ."

"On a bottle of ink?"

"No," he laughed, "I was feeding the first run . . ."

"For goodness' sake, talk English."

"Well," desperately, "while I was putting the papers through the press the clips slipped on one of them and before I could stop the old Babcock she'd wound up tight. Awful mess . . . so I took off the rollers and cleaned 'em."

"And *you're* the awful mess now."

She noted with repugnance how black his fingernails were.

Despite the sulkiness of his reception Kent settled down on the steps near the hammock, with a sigh of satisfaction.

"That positively feels good," he said. "I've been working like a dog."

"But it's scarcely time to commence working yet," said Valentine. She was thinking of the nine o'clock opening hour customary in the opulent offices of her friends.

"Oh, my job began while you were sleeping," her grimy visitor explained. "Poor old Pharaoh is swamped with the extra work of getting out this special edition for your father. He didn't get the forms ready for the first run until two o'clock this morning. Then he woke me up to run them off while he had a bit of rest. I was bunking on a camp couch in the front office."

It all seemed quite foolish and unnecessary to Valentine, and she said so.

"Well, it *is* a bit extraordinary, I'll admit." Just then to Kent the most extraordinary feature of all was the realization that he could feel so healthfully fresh and good natured at eight o'clock in the morning after five solid hours of irksome labor. "But look here, Val, there's no use being cross about it. Of course, I'm beastly sorry about the ankle, and you being interned here in this social wilderness. But a bargain's a bargain, and I'm living up to my end, like a Sunday school hero. The Spartan youth with the wolf in his jeans had nothing on me—only my wolf seems to be at the door."

"It wasn't a wolf . . . it was a fox," proclaimed Valentine.

"The only difference is a fox is smarter, and harder to keep out. But seriously, Val" . . . he turned full towards her now and his bantering tone gave way to earnestness . . . "remember what I told you of the Bishop's farewell lecture about 'jelling'?"

She remembered.

"He said I'd been boiling long enough and needed to 'jell.' You sort of agreed with him. Well, I've jelled a whole lot since I came to Farewell. Seems as if I've settled down and found myself most surprisingly . . . at least it surprises me." He doubled his ink smudged right arm and with the fingers of his left hand felt the muscles. "It isn't just my body that's hardened up, either. It's the rest of me. I've found something to do and I mean to do it."

"Yes?" said Valentine, with mild interest.

Then Kent broached the purpose of his early morning call. He told her in a straightforward way of what he had found at Lost Lake, and of what his idea could mean to the segregation, and the settlers upon it. He also told her that he knew there was not enough water in Welcome River to care for the present segregation, let alone the proposed South Unit; and he explained discreetly his confidence that Alton Pennoyer was unaware of the water shortage, having doubtless been misled by crooked flowage reports. The girl readily grasped the main facts that Kent believed there was not enough water in Welcome River for the needs of her father's irrigation enterprise, and that if the flow from this Lost Lake of his could be turned into the river the defect would be remedied.

"Why don't you tell Dads about it?" she asked.

He hesitated a moment before replying.

"There are two reasons. In the first place, as I said, I don't believe your father knows anything about the water shortage . . ."

"Who does?" Valentine interrupted.

"Well, I know that Failing does and I believe . . ." Again he hesitated.

"Yes, go on," she insisted.

". . . If you must know, the chap at the bottom of it, to my notion, is that fashion plate friend of yours with the bonny braes, Max Welton . . ."

"Just because you're jealous is no reason to insult a . . . a *real* friend of mine," Valentine flamed up.

"Excuse me," he said quietly. And to himself, "Jealous? Oh, Lord!"

"You say you don't believe Dads knows . . . why don't you tell him, then?" She repeated her query sharply.

"I would if it were only he I'd have to deal with. But when a fellow has a good hand he doesn't show his cards until the bets are made. . . . I'm going to file on the water rights at Lost Lake and get them sewed up before I tell what I have." His jaw squared perceptibly. "Then I'll be in shape to make this blessed B. I. C. come to terms —my terms."

"You mean you'll fight father?" The color in her cheeks heightened.

"No," he hesitated, "I don't want to . . . I

won't do that . . . if he will only meet me half way."

"*Meet you half way!*" Valentine's lips curled contemptuously. Her pride was pricked by the absurd notion of this arrogant youth daring to suggest that her father, Alton Pennoyer, should come to him for terms! It was preposterous, and made her all at once thoroughly angry.

"The point is, Valentine," he continued matter-of-factly and feeling very sure of himself now, "that to put this thing over the way it must be handled, I have to break my bargain, at least a little bit."

"It's no bargain of mine," she said curtly.

"Call it anything you like—at least it's the rules of the game I set out to play for this year, just to see if I could play fair and win out. And now I want to break one of 'em—and I've come for your permission."

She offered no encouragement.

"In a few days now I'm going to file on Lost Lake . . . it's a matter of posting some papers up there and taking some others to Salem. That's just the beginning. I'll have to do a lot of improvement work to keep the water rights, if they are contested, which probably they will be. And it takes money to pay for that sort of thing. The rule I want to break," he continued quite gravely, "is the one about money. You know I agreed not to use a dollar but what I earned during the year. Now, I want to draw some from the East—

and Valentine, it's to save a bunch of poor devils out there in the sagebrush who don't begin to know the trouble they're getting into."

"Well?" Valentine's voice was quite colorless. Inwardly she was boiling, and yet at the same time she had a queer consciousness of a desire to laugh aloud; it was so ridiculously unnecessary for this matter-of-fact everyday young man to take the quixotic "rules" so seriously.

"Do you mind?"

His persistency annoyed her afresh.

"Mind?" she flared. "Certainly *not*. I don't care what you do—it's nothing to me!"

"Nothing?"

"David Kent." Her voice shook ominously. "I'm sick and tired of it all."

"You're sick. True enough . . . I'm sorry, Val."

"I'm *not* sick. Don't patronize me." Sympathy only aggravated. . . . "But it's enough to make anyone sick. Why on earth are you puttering around with all this tomfoolery? Where is it getting you? Is it fair to me? As far as I can see you spent most of the summer with this Crete person . . ." The second she said it she wished the words unuttered; but they were gone now, so she plunged on. "You insult my friend; you stir up trouble for my father, and now you actually ask me if I object to your making more trouble for him."

The girl collected herself.

"I'm going home next week." There was a wealth of meaning, almost of invitation, in the announcement.

But Kent did not rise to the occasion; at least he didn't rise in just the way he probably was expected to. Getting to his feet he came over to the hammock, looking down upon the girl as she lay there.

"Valentine, when will you marry me?" She regarded him steadily, too much a thoroughbred to waver.

"*When?*" she mocked.

He nodded, as much as to say, "That's exactly what I mean."

"When will *you* give up . . . this?"

He was tense; all at once it seemed to him he had reached an unexpected crisis. Yet he was able to answer the question with another, and smilingly.

"Will you . . . if I do give up?"

The gray eyes looked into the brown ones, seeing very little of what was just before them and much of what was hidden far beyond. Then all at once they wavered and dropped. Valentine suddenly, surely realized that a new certainty had been born in her heart from its many uncertainties— and that contradictory certainty was that she was *uncertain*.

Kent, watching her face and the new doubts written there, intuitively realized that he would get no answer then—realized, too, that the girl who so long had idled before the gateway of decision now found her heart unwilling to go further when finally her foot was placed upon its threshold.

And instead of utterly casting him down that realization somehow left him strangely satisfied. A feeling inexplicably akin to relief flashed through him. And subconsciously realizing this, David Kent was sorely puzzled.

CHAPTER XX

PI

"I WONDER," said Miranda, when she and Pharaoh quit their work at the *Pioneer* shop to go to Farewell Inn for supper, "I wonder where David is."

It was time for Kent to put in an appearance, for they required his help to make the three remaining runs on the press early that night. Everything was ready for this final step in the preparation of Failing's special edition. Four pages were already locked up, the two heavy chases, each with its two pages, resting on edge beside the press. The other four pages of type were made up upon the imposing stone, ready to have these same chases fitted around them when the printing of the initial run was completed.

It was close to seven o'clock when the editor and his "staff" left the building and night had already settled down.

"B-r-r-r-r!" he chattered, taking Miranda's arm. "It's mighty chilly, Hon."

"Yes, and likely to be colder. See how black it looks."

Through the gathering gloom they still could see the outline of the Cascade Range to the west with an ominous dark mass of clouds hanging close above the mountains.

"It's snowing up there," said Pharaoh, sighing wearily. "That means the end of the summer, and here we're scarcely into October. It's a God-forsaken short season at best."

As they sat in the fly-specked dining-room of the inn Failing entered.

"How's it coming?" he asked curtly.

"Fine," replied Pharaoh, gulping the dregs of his coffee. "We're going back now to put the last runs on the press. The bundles you want will be ready not much after midnight, I think."

The manager grunted his approval. "I'll drop in later," he said, and rolled away.

"And now," said Pharaoh to Miranda, "I'll just take you around to the Company House and leave you with Crete and Miss Pennoyer for a bit of a rest. They'll welcome company, I reckon . . . a queer combination those two . . . like a French doll and a Teddy bear—'cept in looks," he chuckled.

She objected, but for once to no avail, and to the Company House she was taken, whence Pharaoh went on his way to the *Pioneer*. He could see an uncertain light through the shop windows as he approached. "That's David," he thought, "starting work."

When the slight form of the editor and the

ample outlines of his wife became lost in the gloom as they proceeded toward the inn for their supper, a figure emerged from the shadow of a juniper tree near the *Pioneer* building.

Seeing the coast clear the figure advanced quickly and opened the unlocked door of the editorial sanctum. Once within, the man appeared to be familiar with his surroundings and to know exactly the purpose of his unbidden entrance. On his way to the printshop he brushed by the small safe which Pharaoh had once taken on a bad advertising account and wherein he always firmly intended to lock up each night the cashbook and subscription records of the *Pioneer*, a laudable intention actually fulfilled with methodical irregularity. To-night as usual the records and the slim cashbook were on the counter instead of in the safe.

"Had I better pull a little real robbery to make it realistic?" the marauder questioned aloud, and then after considering this unique proposition for a moment he chuckled and knelt down beside the safe. A few turns of the combination, a few soft metal clicks, and the heavy door swung open. Whereupon the cracksman, instead of taking something from the safe, put something into it, in the shape of a note which he scrawled with cool deliberation, lighting his epistle with the glare of a tiny electric flash. Then this unprofessional Raffles shut the door and turned to the business of his call.

The flashlight played for an instant over the Babcock press. Then it focused upon the two forms of type, set on edge in the chases close at hand.

In the mechanics of printing, type after being set in a "stick" is assembled on large flat stones and the page or form to be printed is "made up," which is by way of saying that it is put into final shape for the printing process. Then a steel frame called a "chase" is laid over the "form." This done, the form is literally wedged into the surrounding chase, finally being "locked" with ingenious contrivances called "quoins," which are adjusted in such a way as to make a great tension from one side of the chase to the other. It is this pressure which keeps all the myriad particles of type in place. Then the heavy form, with its many pounds of lead, is lifted and placed upon the press for printing. It is during this process of moving a form that the greatest printshop tragedies sometimes occur. For if the quoins are not tightened to the $n'th$ degree, or if some portion of the type is not properly put in place or justified,—or if, for instance, a printer slips and knocks the precious burden upon some corner, or lets it fall,—catastrophe superlative ensues with appalling completeness. All at once the orderly flat form of type is a mess of metal upon the floor; the chase, instead of framing a neat plane of type faces, surrounds thin air; and there remains a heartbreaking work of hours or even days to put in order again the scrambled litter of type, which printers call "pi."

It was such a form, locked in its chase, that the flashlight fell upon. It was, or would be when printed, four full pages of James Failing's special edition of the Farewell *Pioneer*.

Those particular forms, however, would never be printed. For the masked marauder, placing his foot in the middle of the nearest one, pressed against it until the type gave way and the whole mass of metal shattered into a pyramid upon the floor. Thereupon the visitor repeated the process with the second form, giving this one a brisk kick which sent the leaden type clattering out of the chase. Next he turned his attention to the other forms upon the nearby stone. A hearty shove at one edge and four pages more of *Pioneer* special edition crashed to the floor in hopeless pi.

It was that dull thud which Pharaoh heard as he approached the shop.

Simultaneously with the destruction of the last form the front door of the office opened. The masked man heard it and quickly dodged into the shadow behind a pile of news stock. Footsteps, after a moment of silence, cautiously advanced. The newcomer was now but a half dozen feet from the man in hiding, and the latter could hear the sound of a match being struck, followed by a flicker of light.

But the match never fully ignited. It fell from Pharaoh's hands when suddenly a dazzling electric flash was thrown full in his eyes, for the moment blinding him.

"Oh, it's *you*," the voice sounded distinctly relieved. Then the flash was extinguished and with a rush the interloper made for the door. Beside it he paused for an instant.

"Look at the safe." This time the voice was very gruff. With this enigmatical advice the stranger was lost in the night.

Afterward, thinking it over, Pharaoh felt sure that he had heard a farewell chuckle. But just then his one certainty was that he would find the safe rifled. However, that troubled him little, the barrenness of its interior striking him as an admirable joke upon the pilferer.

"Why didn't he try a real safe, instead of a printer's," he smiled to himself, as he groped his way into the press room.

Standing upon a stool, the editor struck another match and lit one of the hanging lamps which furnished illumination for the shop. All at once, as he stepped down to the floor, an astounding sight met his eyes. In one glance he saw the mass of caved-in type beside the press and the other forms in a littered heap beneath the stone. Instantly the meaning of it struck home to him. Seeing and understanding the completeness of the wreck, Pharaoh's heart suddenly went cold with the desolating shock, and he staggered and fell to the floor in a faint.

The third man that evening to open the *Pioneer's*

office door was James Failing who "dropped in" to see how his newspaper progeny was progressing. Puzzled at finding the office dark, he moved toward the light in the rear. In the outer circle of that light, midway between it and the office, he all but stumbled on something which made him start.

"What the devil . . ." he ejaculated, and then discovered that the dark something was the form of Pharaoh Jones, stretched out upon the floor.

The sound of Failing's voice startled the editor, who had been lying there for perhaps ten minutes, into semi-consciousness.

"What's wrong here, anyway?" continued the manager, querulously, leaning over Pharaoh, who in a few seconds was able to sit up.

"What the devil's wrong? . . . that's what I want to know."

For answer Pharaoh weakly stretched out his hand, still inarticulate. Following its direction the manager saw the jumbled heaps of metal.

"What's the idea . . . what's all that litter?" Lacking a printer's eye he did not realize that the leaden piles were the gravestones of his cherished journalistic effort.

"It's the special edition . . . there on the floor," explained Pharaoh weakly. "The forms have been all smashed up . . . there's nothing left but pi . . . ."

"You mean," the manager cleared his throat with an obvious effort, "you mean the paper's been wrecked? . . . you can't finish the job?"

Pharaoh nodded.

"Hell and damnation!" Failing blazed into fury, then all at once was silent, too bitterly angry even for words. "Who did it?" Pharaoh shrank uneasily.

"I . . . I . . ." That was as far as his voice could carry him.

"*You?* You don't mean to say you had a hand in it?"

The impossibility of such a supposition revived the editor. "God, no!" he expostulated.

"Who was it, then? Do you know . . . out with it!"

Just then the crisp cannonade of hoofs galloping across the bridge which spanned Welcome River came distinctly to the ears of the two men, facing each other there in the partial gloom of the pillaged printshop, and the sound brought the same idea to both.

"That's he," thought Pharaoh. "Why, *why* did he do it?"

Failing spoke his thought aloud. "The dirty whelp," he sputtered. "I saw him with a horse at Frost's barn early this evening—so he's turned outlaw. Well, we'll cook his goose for sure this time." Then he swung upon Pharaoh. "The paper's gone to hell? No chance to get it out now?"

"Not for a week, at least." The editor spoke numbly.

The manager eyed the wreckage and the *Pioneer's*

owner in turn, and his glance was anything but pleasant.

"I don't know what's your part in this, but I'll find out soon enough. This much is 'sure . . . that troublemaking side-kicker of yours, Master Davy Kent, is in for some regular trouble himself. He's responsible and it's going to be easy to hang it on him. You can't break into buildings and destroy property and get away with it . . . there's plenty in the Pen at Salem for less crimes."

CHAPTER XXI

CRETE HAS A PLAN

VALENTINE PENNOYER, Crete, and Miranda were grouped about the open fire at the Company House when the manager stormed in upon them.

"Everything going well with your paper, I hope?" Valentine inquired languidly.

"*Well?*" he fairly snorted, glaring down at the girl. Then he subsided into the nearest chair, with a nervous attempt at laughter. "Not exactly. At least it didn't look so awfully fine when I last saw it . . . that is, unless you like printer's pi."

"Printer's pie?" echoed Valentine, completely puzzled.

The sewing dropped from Miranda's hands. "You don't mean to say he dropped the forms?"

"No indeed," he reassured her sourly. "Nobody dropped anything. Only an earthquake came along all of a sudden and busted things wide open. The net result is the grandest little mess you ever saw."

Miranda stared at him, horrified. "Yes," he nodded, singling her out, "the whole thing is wrecked . . . the forms were either kicked to pieces or dumped on the floor . . . there isn't any more special edition than a rabbit . . ."

"Poor Pharaoh!" Miranda burst into tears. The hard work wasted, the money earned but now not to be received, the pity of it all—that was her first thought.

"Poor Pharaoh?" The manager's voice broke into a disgusted tremolo. "How about *me?* . . . that's what I want to know. Where do *I* get off? What'll the ol'—er—that is, what'll Mr. Pennoyer think? " Then, almost piteously, he poured out his tale to Alton Pennoyer's daughter, telling her of the wrecked special edition.

"Who did it?" Up to then Crete Colton had remained silent.

Failing started to speak, then halted with his mouth half open, spellbound by a sudden appalling realization.

"One of those anarchist settlers, I suppose?" offered Valentine, a bit grandly.

Failing's objective anger had all at once turned to subjective pity. His immediate ambition was to escape from the presence of his employer's daughter, whose next act, he feared, would be the discovery that her fiancé (he supposed Kent to be practically that) was at the bottom of the trouble.

Which was exactly what Valentine did do. Her curiosity aroused, she meant to know all there was to know.

"Yes, Mr. Failing . . . tell us who did it," she insisted.

And Failing miserably cleared his throat: "David Kent!"

The blood rushed to Valentine's face. Crete's expression changed not a whit, unless she became a shade paler; Miranda stopped her crying.

"Of course," the manager added, a bit weakly, "it isn't proved yet" . . . Valentine was looking straight at him, making him feel even more uncomfortable . . . "but . . . well, it's practically certain. I saw him get a horse about six o'clock . . ."

"You mean," Valentine spoke deliberately, in a far-away voice, "that you're sure Mr. Kent wrecked the paper?"

Failing nodded. "Someone rode away on horseback just after I found Jones. On the way over here I scouted around a bit and discovered where a horse had been tied to a tree near by—and I also found *this*."

From his pocket he took a crumpled empty envelope. Valentine, silently and imperiously, held out her hand, and the manager gave it to her. The envelope bore a typewritten address, "Mr. David Kent, Farewell, Ore." She sat fingering it a moment, silent, looking straight before her. Then the gray eyes returned to the telltale bit of paper and she noticed something else about it. The return card of the State Water Master was in the corner.

Failing made a move to go. He felt a storm imminent and that he might be the object of its onslaught, not because he deserved it but because he was bearing witness against Kent. The merits of the case didn't matter, he realized.

But Valentine did the totally unexpected, and the way she did it was characteristic.

"Do you know where Mr. Kent has gone?" Apparently she had accepted his guilt and felt there was no need for comment. From the tightening of her lips and a certain hardening of the handsome face it could be gathered that the outstanding fact in her estimation was that Kent had turned upon her father in open warfare—outlawry existed to be crushed. . . . Crete Colton, alone in that room, read the aristocratic face aright.

Failing did not know and said so.

"Well, I do," Valentine announced coolly. "He's on his way to Lost Lake now, I imagine."

"Lost Lake?"

"Yes. Listen." And in a businesslike way— the very tones seemed inherited from her father— she recounted Kent's plans for securing the water rights at Lost Lake just as he had told her, in confidence, that morning. "Only to-day," she concluded, "he said he intended going up there immediately to post his notices, after which he'd file at Salem. Aren't there certain blanks necessary?"

The manager nodded.

"Well, don't you see?" she held up the envelope from the State Water Master's office, "the blanks came in this. He probably just got them."

There was absolute silence.

"The thing to do," said Failing, "is to swear out a warrant—we'll jail him for destroying property."

Valentine considered the proposition for a moment.

"Yes, that's right enough . . . but how about the Lake?"

Failing grinned, a plan unfolding in his mind.

"Why shouldn't *we* file on that water, Miss Pennoyer?" The wine-colored eyes warmed. "I'll rush a couple of the boys up there right away . . . they can beat Kent to it, get their filings posted before he's wise to what's going on, and be back here in time for the stage day-after-to-morrow morning."

"But how about Da—Mr. Kent?"

"Don't you see . . . when he comes back and starts out for Shaniko we'll nab him . . . the warrant'll be all ready. Even if he dodges Farewell and cuts cross country to Roundville it'll be easy to catch him. Anyway, he couldn't possibly get past Shaniko—we'd have 'em ready for him there, sure."

Valentine joined in these man-hunting plans keenly. She felt very much alive, very coolly determined—very much like Alton Pennoyer in action, had she known it.

"But supposing he gets to Salem some other way, and beats us?" She did not propose to have any slip.

"Impossible. Salem's just about due west across the Cascades. The only way to get there is by the railroad clear up to the Columbia and then around by Portland. As for me," Failing added, "I'll start for Portland in the morning to tell your father how things are coming."

"And I'll sit right down now and write a letter for you to take him," replied Valentine. "After all, it looks as if we'll get something worth much more than that paper our friend smashed up. Will you excuse me, Miss Colton?"

But Crete was gone. As the manager was unfolding his plans she had slipped out.

"She's gone over to help Pharaoh," Miranda said. "If you don't mind, I'll stay here until he comes for me."

"Oh, certainly." And, securing a pad, Valentine commenced her letter.

"*That's what she calls love!*" Out in the cool gloom of the night, Crete aired her indignant opinion. All the generous loyalty in her nature was ablaze with resentment.

She found Pharaoh seated in the unlighted *Pioneer* office, his head buried in his arms on the desk. Without a word to him, Crete lit the office lamp, started a fire in the stove, and perched herself upon a stool.

Crete Has a Plan 213

Presently the editor roused himself, raising eyes suspiciously red. "Well?" he said miserably.

"Pharaoh, cheer up! . . . *please.*" The very tone was steadying. If it were to be a contest of feminine wits there'd be no emotional weakness on this side. "Now tell me all about it."

"There's nothing to tell," he sighed wearily. "It's just all messed up in there—everything pied. When I started into the shop" . . . he was getting himself together . . . "someone flashed a light in my face . . ."

"Who?"

"I don't know," he lied loyally.

"Failing does."

"He suspects . . . he can't be *sure.*"

"That's the worst of it—he is sure. He found this out by a tree where a horse had been tethered." She handed him the envelope addressed to Kent which she had quietly pocketed, unnoticed, while the manager and Valentine talked.

Pharaoh's manner in receiving it showed Crete he already knew who had wrought the mischief. Then the girl picked up the envelope and lifting the stove cover thrust it into the fire. "Exhibit A vanishes!" she announced. "If we must have melodrama let's burn the evidence in the most accepted style."

"He said something about the safe . . ." Pharaoh just then remembered it.

"Oh! . . . I wonder if he did a little regular burglarizing, for appearance's sake?"

However, they found the safe fast shut with no evidence of tampering.

"You're positive he spoke about it?" She was puzzled.

"Yes. It was something about 'looking in the safe,' I'm sure."

"Well, look then."

In the safe they found this message scrawled upon a bit of copy paper:

"Starting to-night for the Lake to post filing notice. Keep absolutely mum.

"D. K."

"All of which is no news over at the Company House," remarked Crete, after reading it.

"Eh, what's that?" Just then Pharaoh was thinking of the snow squall which he and Miranda had seen sweeping over the mountains. And Kent—extraordinary David—was headed for the highlands on horseback, alone.

Crete told him, then, what had happened at the Company House.

"What's next?" he asked lamely.

"Easy enough to see," she replied. "As soon as David gets back they'll arrest him—he seems not to have figured on that. And in the meantime Failing's men . . . I suppose he's starting Callier right now . . . will have posted his notices and probably torn down David's. The rest is simple . . . while they're holding David here for trial, or however it's fixed, Callier will dodge down to Salem and . . . well, there you are!"

"I'm a bit puzzled," she continued after a brief silence, "as to just what charge they'll bring in connection with David's little house-wrecking bee here . . . but trust them to rig up something that'll stick at least long enough to put him out of the running. That's easy . . . and of course I suppose he *did* commit a crime."

Pharaoh had some notions on that head himself —notions which had been fomenting as the girl talked. But he kept silent.

Then some sudden new angle of the situation struck Crete, causing her to act in unprecedented fashion. Smilingly she balanced on the arm of the precarious editorial chair and putting her strong young arms about the editorial neck she gave astonished Pharaoh the nicest kind of a kiss which it is possible for a sensible girl of twenty-six to give a fatherly invalid close to fifty.

"Pharaoh, you old dear," she chortled, "it's not going to happen that way at all!"

The girl was radiant with some secret inspiration.

"There's nothing to . . . to laugh about." He tried to be gruff.

"But there will be!"

And she unfolded a plan to Pharaoh which left the emaciated editor alternately experiencing throes of elated approval and vehemently protesting against the proposal with a sincerity which was as heartfelt as it was ineffectual.

CHAPTER XXII

ON THE TRAIL, AND OFF

Dawn unfolded slowly that October morning upon a world cold and gray. Underfoot the ground was crisp with frost and a fairy blanket of hoary white overlaid the needle carpet of the forest floor and wove spidery crystal webs among the robust foliage of the manzanita. The pine tops sighed uneasily in their lofty intimacy with the threatening skies. Sun-up time came and passed, but no sun appeared and no autumn blue brightened the heavens. Instead, the strengthening daylight showed legionary ragged clouds, frayed by the hastening winds, surging southward.

That unpromising dawn found two horses with their riders winding slowly along a blazed trail westerly from Farewell.

At the top of a rise, where the sparsity of trees upon a neighboring rocky ridge afforded a fairly unrestricted view, the first horseman stopped, allowing his companion to range up beside him. From his mackinaw pocket the leader, who was Dad Trumble, extracted his pipe, lit it, and puffed deliberately as he took stock of the warnings in the sky.

"Cold?" he asked.

His companion looked anything but cold, despite the chill of the hour. A trapper's hat of fur, illegally fashioned from forbidden beaver, a fine thick coat made of sheepskin with the leather out and the wool in, and buccaroo's leather chaps from waist to ankle afforded protection against the elements quite as thorough as could be devised for horseback wear.

"You look like a bygod sheepherding Basque," laughed Dad, taking in the details of the outfit. "There ain't a sheep dog in the country wouldn't claim you as a friend. But never mind the looks —that's the clear quill in rigs when it comes to cold and wet . . . which I reckon it's coming, pronto."

"Snow?" Crete Colton's voice was just as freshly comfortable as it had been the preceding evening when she unfolded her plan to Pharaoh in the *Pioneer* office.

"Yep—and plenty of it." The old woodsman sniffed the air. "Can't you *smell* it? It's snowing up above now . . . we'll be into it soon. I'm only hoping it won't come down so plumb hard we can't follow tracks."

She caught his meaning, and both of them were silent for a space.

"Isn't it *quiet*—so wonderfully still!" The girl's exclamation was hushed as if attuned to the surrounding silence of Nature. And, indeed, the timberlands were infinitely noiseless, with never a sound to break the dead, pulseless hush except the low moan of the treetops protesting in the upper air, a symphony of soft movement which made the quiet appear even the more profound.

Dad nodded. "You can actually *hear* it, she's so *in*ternally still. That's always how it is in the woods before a storm, 'specially these first fall blows. Well, let's mosey . . . it's a long way."

A little later he pulled his horse up in a sandy opening where the dry ground was entirely unfrozen and so suitably receptive for tracks. As the girl came alongside of him the old man pointed out fresh hoofmarks, showing clearly in the sand.

"It's Dave. He's ahead of us all right. Two or three times down the line I reckoned I seen his trail but I couldn't be sartain sure what with the frozen ground and the bad light. How th' lad managed to keep going in the night I don't see. He couldn't have made much time to speak of, anyway. I callate we've picked up a couple of hours on him, sure . . . and right here is where we gain another, just for good measure. See that bald ridge yonder in line with the hump on the Chief where it shows through the cloud?" She saw the point, probably three miles distant, but separated by a broken, billowing valley of timber, thickets, and rocky outpourings.

"Lost Lake's over yonder. This trail we're on

On the Trail, And Off

goes way up around the west end of the big draw by Grassy Lake, an' it takes a matter of seven miles or so to get over there, when a crow'd make it in three. We ain't crows, but we'll try the short cut."

He added that it would be well to tighten the cinches as the going would be rough. So they dismounted, enjoyed a welcome stretch, ate a sandwich, and readjusted saddle blankets and cinches.

"Dad, I've been puzzling for the last hour," Crete announced as they remounted.

"What's the puzzle—what we're going ter do?"

"No," she laughed, "I know that all right."

"More'n I do, then," he grumbled, quizzically.

"You promised to sail under sealed orders—and obey them," she reminded him directly. "You know the penalty for mutiny?"

"Yes'm. Reckon I'd be allowed to go back home where I belong and get a reg'lar sleep!"

She laughed heartily. "Poor old Dad, it's a shame . . ."

"Poor *old* nothing . . . this bird isn't ripe for an indignant old folks' home yet a while. Dodgast it, I can work th' legs off any one of the male chickens they raise these days an' when it comes to . . ." but he saw she was laughing at him and subsided with a snort. As a parting shot, he added, "What does get my goat is how you can keep agoin' an' never let me in on the plans—durn me if you ain't got the tarnation record when it comes to women for keepin' a secret . . ." inviting silence; then—"Well, Boss—you're it all right—what's the question?"

"Where's Mr. Callier? He must have left Farewell about the time we did."

"Reckon I know," he replied, evidently having thought out the problem for himself. "You see, that Callier ain't really acquainted with this country. This here trail we come on is the regular old Ringo Trail but it ain't the one the rangers use to get to th' lake—that's over yonder, where we're going now, t'other side of this draw. They cut the new trail to have more ways of fire patrolling in summer. T'other's the trail that Callier's usin'."

"And I don't suppose they're hurrying a bit," added the girl, questioningly. "They think all they've got to do is to reach the lake some time to-day and then get back to Farewell comfortably for to-morrow morning's stage."

"'Zactly." Clucking to his horse, Dad led the way down a steep pitch, with Fantan following his leader heroically while Crete leaned far back in her cowboy saddle, her chap-clad legs raised nearly to Fantan's ears in an effort to keep her body reasonably vertical, while her arms hung at her sides, with the loose-jointed ease of western riding ways.

As they worked their way laboriously down the slopes, skirting now bowlder-strewn slides or forcing their way through tamarack thickets, the snow squalls commenced. First came intermittent gusts of damp-scented wind and then dashes of snow, driven cuttingly by a north wind which shortly steadied down to the business of bringing a blizzard with disquieting zeal. Then, with the freakish mannerisms of mountain storms, the wind abated for a time and the snow came faster in moist fluffy flakes which fell almost straight and so amazingly thick that every sight was blotted out except the blurred, downward-moving wall of whitish gray. That introductory heavy fall continued for but a few minutes, when the wind resumed its boreal romping, swirling and tearing the white curtain phantastically.

Enough descended in the first deluge to coat the ground and laden the branches with moist whiteness which slapped dankly in their faces and smothered horses and riders as they crowded through small growth and low-lying limbs. It became colder, too, and forthwith the moisture upon them froze, so that the thoroughly soaked outer wooliness of Crete's chaps became brittle and crackly, and the pinto's abbreviated mane stuck up icily like a stiff bath brush.

Seldom could they see more than a hundred yards ahead and even then the view embraced nothing more distinctive than a clump of trees, a thicket, or a rocky ridge exactly resembling scores of neighboring trees, thickets, and ridges. A dozen times, as her guide paused to study the landmarks, Crete felt sure that they were lost;

and each time, as Dad again plunged forward with cheering assurance, she marveled anew that he could keep his directions.

Finally they commenced to climb, and soon halted in the lee of a big fallen tree, shattered by lightning.

"We came out jes *egzakly* right," Dad announced with a measure of justifiable pride. "I was a-headin' for this here down tree. It's only a bit of a lift now up to the other trail."

A few minutes later Crete saw a fresh blaze upon a tree trunk—the regulation Forest Service marking for trails, one large blaze with two smaller notches below it.

"Yep," said Dad, when she called his attention to it, "we hit the trail back yonder on that stretch of open ground. Only you didn't notice 'count of the snow coverin' it up."

"Are there any tracks?" She had been worrying about Callier.

"Not *on top* of the snow, anyway," Dad replied good-naturedly. "But here's where I get a look at the ground—if they went by before the snow set in it'll show here."

Dismounting, he examined minutely the trail where for a few feet it was bare of snow beneath the thick branches of a big tamarack.

"Nothing there for a long spell . . . see how a fresh track shows where the dirt's dry?" He led his horse over the bit of dry ground, the hoofs scuffling up dark clods of telltale brown earth.

"So our friends is somewhere behind us . . . an' not so very far, neither, 'less I miss my guess. That is, unless they're afraid o' gettin' their lovely noses frostbit."

Crete considered the possibility.

"No, they wouldn't turn back," she opined, "it's a rush order and too important for them to dare lie down."

"An' do yer 'spose Dave perhaps threw up the sponge when the snow commenced gettin' bad?"

"Certainly not!" the reply came instantly, almost reprovingly.

"Thasright," he agreed hastily, with a twinkle she didn't see, "he ain't the quittin' kind." To which he added, to himself, "Nor you, neither."

The timber was behind them now except for scattered stunted stragglers, ghostly forms of white showing grotesquely against the gray middle distance of the ever-falling flakes. Among the trees the storm had seemed less serious and somehow less real. Winding through them, indeed, surrounded by the myriad beauties which come with snowtime in the forest, when each turn brings fresh views of fairylandish delight and each gusty squall is the signal for another shift of scenery, Crete had found it all quite pleasantly theatrical, despite the small hardships of their progress. But there in the open, with the chill breath of the Chief blowing directly upon them, the surroundings became bitterly wintry. The wind howled with an unchecked sweep from the north, chasing recurrent squalls of crowding snowflakes across the upland waste.

They swung the unenthusiastic horses on the way out upon Wickiup Flat which intervened between them and Lost Lake. In summer this is a great rolling bowlder-strewn mountain meadow land, roughly broken up with wide flat surfaces of stone burnished blackly where glaciers of long ago ground across them. Scores of tiny ponds fed by the melting snows of winter and the rains of spring are scattered as chance wills in the cups and depressions of the plateau. They are pretty play lakes in July and August when the summer sky reflects in their surface and brilliant upland flowers bloom about their borders, and the whole expanse of highland is green with coarse mountain grass. But as the horses trudged across the Flat that October day it looked and felt like a bleak Siberian wilderness.

The storm had broken hours earlier up there and the snow lay deep upon the ground. The going for the horses became increasingly difficult, as did finding and following the trail. Indeed, Dad was guided more by his sixth sense of direction and the general "lie of the land" than by any specific beacons, for the occasional cairns and other markings were already pretty thoroughly hidden.

As they reached the point where the trail dipped down to their destination, where Dad had introduced Kent and Rudd to Lost Lake not many weeks before, the old man looked back over the way they had come. Already little swirls of snow were obliterating their tracks.

"I hope ter hell she don't drift bad," he growled.

"Eh? What's that, Dad?"

"Oh, I only was thinkin' that sometimes it's easier to climb a tree than to get down again."

"Is there any danger?"

"No . . . an' yes. It might be that this here pesky storm'll kick up into a reg'lar whopper . . . but that ain't prob'le this early in the year. More'n likely it'll blow itself out 'safternoon. 'Thout she keeps on snowin' good an' proper everything's hunky dory. . . . Most anyone could find his way home. An' now, I 'spose, you want to go down to the bygod lake?"

"Surely . . . and a bit of fire won't feel badly."

"Right you are . . . it won't. But say" . . . he peered at what he could see of Crete's face, hidden as it was by the icy fur of her hat . . . "what's the idee anyway? How long is we to rusticate by this bloomin' open fire o' ours? Don't you think, Skipper, it's 'bout time to loosen up on them sealed orders of yourn . . . even to a bygod . . . well, say a stoker?"

Crete laughed aloud. Dad's perennial good humor was comforting.

"There's no great secret and no doubt you know just as well as I do what we've come for . . . which is simply to help David file on these water rights he wants."

"Oh sure," he echoed, "that's simple as shootin' fish. Only couldn't we have 'complished that there laud'ble end, as the feller sez, by jes' stayin' ter Farewell, cozy-like, 'thout mushing away up here?"

"Oh, of course we might have stayed home . . . and let them arrest David the minute he got back! I'm sure he'd appreciate our help."

"How we goin' to stop them pinchin' him?"

"I'm not sure," the girl replied, "only at least we can warn him. Perhaps he'll be able to give them the slip and beat them to Salem. And I've got another notion. In that saddlebag" . . . she laid a gauntleted hand upon it . . . "There are filing papers to post myself. . . . Pharaoh dug them up and showed me just what to do last night before we started. If anything should happen so that David can't post his own notice or if he shouldn't be able to get away to Salem to make the filing h i m s e l f, why, I thought I'd do some filing on my own hook."

As they descended in the lee of the Chief its great bulk effectually broke the fury of the storm, while in the cuplike hollow where Lost Lake cuddled in close at the foot of the talus slopes they found far less snow had fallen than out upon the Flat.

They skirted the north side of the lake between the shore line and the abrupt mountain whose heights were hidden in the gray mist of the descending flakes. Here and there tufts of meadow grass rose above the snow, to the distraction of the horses. Most of the lake was frozen, distinguishable only as a smooth flat surface of white set in a less regular white mounting. Only near the outlet at the western end where a current moved had the ice failed to form, and there the patch of open water showed jet black, a thin pale mist hanging close over it and the persistent flakes vanishing interminably as they reached the inky water. The tamaracks where Dad and his companions had camped in August now drooped beneath their wintry burden. Their boughs were close and strong, however, and where the clump stood thickest considerable spaces of ground remained bare.

In such a spot the riders halted, and in a few minutes a little fire was blazing briskly. From a saddlebag Dad then extracted a battered lard pail quite devoid of shapeliness but, as he forthwith ascertained with relieved satisfaction, unleaking. The same repository yielded a tiny sack of sugar, a piece of soiled rag tightly tied around something which, it developed, was tea, a loaf of bread esconced in a copy of the *Pioneer*, and, lastly, a greasy brown package. There were also two dented tin cups.

"Tea," said the old woodsman, "is th' clear quill on a trip . . . it's hot an' comfortin' and don't weigh nothing at all. Tastes fine even 'thout canned cow an's plenty good enough 'thout sugar . . . beats coffee three ways when you're packing."

"But Dad" . . . she asked, with a chunk of bread poised midway to her mouth . . . "what's the mystery in there?"

"Mowich," Dad's mouth was literally "too full for utterance" . . . at least of the clearly intelligible order . . . "Wansome?"

"Is it to eat?"

"Yerbetyer." Unrolling the greasy paper he displayed some slivers of soiled looking dry meat. He held one up; its appearance was midway between that of a smoked herring and a scrap of cowhide. "Jerky—can't be beat . . . the tastingest stuff ever you set yer teeth on and it everlastingly sticks to the ribs."

She took a sliver gingerly. Its odor was in keeping with its appearance. But the taste was all that Dad claimed . . . jerked venison is at any time a treat for a healthy appetite, and in the surroundings of that snowbound meal it seemed positively the essence of gastronomic luxury.

They were eating in comfortable silence when the girl happened to look through the branches along the way they had come. Another horseback figure was advancing up the trail.

"Dad, look!" she whispered. "Is it David?"

The old man studied the horseman for a minute, then spat disgustedly in the fire. "No . . . it's that damn Callier." A new thought disturbed him. "Say, Girl, it ain't exactly pomme de tair, as the dagoes say, for you to be galavanting round up here with me . . . even tho' I am old enough

On the Trail, And Off 229

to be yer grandad . . . leastwise, not for skunks like him ter talk about."

That sort of thing never troubled Crete in the least, but she saw the point nevertheless.

"I'll hide if you think best . . . there'll be plenty to talk about before this party's through, anyway."

So before the approaching horseman was near enough to detect anything, the girl and her pony had slipped into the depths of the thicket and the old man had contrived to obliterate the tell-tale tracks so that they were indistinguishable, at least on casual observation. The falling snow beyond the shelter of the trees had already cared for this detail so far as the back trail was concerned.

"Howdy, Callier."

The sales manager returned Dad's greeting. Then he sat silently regarding the old man, his face as expressionless as the snowfield behind him.

"Seen anything of young Kent?"

"I reckoned you'd be waiting for him," Callier replied dryly, looking around at the snow-burdened trees and frozen lake. "Kind of a cozy place to wait, ain't it? But say, Ol' Timer" . . . he spit largely upon the snow, "you might as well pack up and beat it. Mister Kent ain't a-going to show up to-day."

"Thasso?" Dad's expression was as disinterested as the other's. "'Z fer me, I can't say he made no rendevooz. I was jes' out prospecting a bit and got caught up in this blow."

"Then you won't miss him. But as one of his pet friends you'll be interested to know he's locked up at Farewell. At least" . . . he compromised with the truth, "he's arrested, safe enough. I'll be going now . . . and here's hoping you enjoy your visit."

Dad watched Callier as he rode down to the outlet of the lake. He saw him go to a tree standing close beside the little stream and unfold something white which he took from his pocket. Then he kicked around in the snow at the water's edge, found a small stone, and using it as a hammer tacked the paper to the tree trunk. That done, he turned eastward and rode back the way he had come.

CHAPTER XXIII

THE BRAIN STORM

WHEN he started from Farewell after the escapade in the Pioneer shop, Kent had intended to spend the night at Crowder's logging camp, a couple of miles from town. But while there were no stars in the sky it was not excessively dark and the rider found the wood road so easy to follow, the air so pleasantly crisp, his horse so willing, and his own thoughts so exhilarated that by the time the camp was reached he abandoned the plan of sleeping there and decided to push on.

The notion of riding all night struck his fancy. The sensation of action and adventure—the realization that he was embarking upon something difficult and a bit dangerous—was stimulating. The entire undertaking appeared pleasingly picturesque.

Shortly after dawn, while he was walking to get the saddle stiffness out of his legs, a powdery snowflake flecked his hand, and as if at a preconceived signal, the white downpour commenced. He could see nothing now of the sky above— nothing but the blurred haziness of millions of falling flakes. In the upper grayness, the treetops whined ominously.

Kent looked over his shoulder at Pedro and Pedro looked at him, with his ears cocked forward inquiringly. The horse whinnied, as much as to say, "It's time to get along—preferably home."

"All right, Peter, my lad!" Brushing the gathering film of snow from the leather he swung into the saddle and to Pedro's sorrow kept his head to the west.

The further they went the heavier lay the snow upon the ground. Gradually, as the wind awoke, the orderly, lazy fall became an angry white deluge which swirled and whistled through the branches, beating against horse and rider with increasing bitterness.

"If I thought it would keep up I'd be inclined to quit." Kent talked his thoughts aloud for the company of it. "But it would be a fool shame to go back after getting this far. . . . I'd feel awfully cheap . . . and then, too, it's likely the last chance to reach the Lake before spring. If I don't make the filing now we can't do a thing until heaven knows when."

If the young man had suspected for an instant that others were already on their way to make filings ahead of him he would have driven on to Lost Lake as fast as Pedro's legs could move, blizzard or no blizzard. But such a possibility did not occur to him.

He did remember, however, that the barren

plateau of Wickiup Flat intervened between him and the Lake, and the more he considered those last few miles in the open the more he realized their difficulties and dangers. It was troublesome enough to keep the trail in the timber and he realized full well how easily it could be lost in the open wastes of the Flat.

"Sloughing around all night in the drifts out there doesn't appeal to me for a cent," he soliloquized.

Already the timber was thinning out and he knew he must be close to the edge of the plain, a fact attested by the increasing ferocity of the wind which swept across the open reaches of the Flat with boreal abandon. The storm seemed growing worse. Kent was bitter cold and Pedro's progress was increasingly half-hearted.

So he compromised with the elements. He neither turned back nor went ahead. Instead he guided Pedro a few rods off the trail to a heavy limbed fir tree towering among a group of lesser neighbors. Beneath its boughs there was shelter from the falling snow, and the thicket partially surrounding it, in a large measure warded off the wind.

Having unsaddled and tied Pedro the wayfarer kindled a fire upon a patch of bare ground and extracted some bulky sandwiches from a saddlebag. The other of the two bags, containing sundry purchases whose mysterious nature had roused the unrequited curiosity of the proprietor of the Farewell Hardware Company, he deposited carefully in the immediate lee of the large tree. Then he stretched out a saddle blanket, fixed the saddle itself as a back rest and arranged himself as comfortably as possible before the fire to await the developments of the storm.

Leon Callier and Jeb Watterson did not leave Farewell until nearly five o'clock that morning, an hour after Dad Trumble and Crete had started. Of the departure of these two, Failing's agents knew nothing, and, secure in the belief that their unsuspecting quarry—and he alone—was somewhere between them and Lost Lake, they made no special effort to hasten.

All at once Callier, who was in the lead, checked his horse and raised his hand warningly. Through a momentary lull in the storm they heard a man's voice, singing.

"That's Kent," said Callier, and then considered plans. "How far are we from the Lake?"

"About three miles, I reckon . . . but from here it is mostly out in the open across Wickiup Flat. It'll be God-awful blowy out there."

"But it oughtn't to be hard to get across?" Callier questioned.

"No-o-o . . . that is, 'tain't usually. There's plenty of monuments along the trail and unless they're drifted over she'd be easy to find. It's mostly level and the going's good."

"Well, look here, Jeb," said Callier. "It seems to me the thing to do is to grab this guy pronto.

It's just a question of which one of us stays with him, while the other goes ahead and does the filing . . . do you think I could find my way all right?"

Jeb, getting the point with unusual celerity, assured his companion he should have little difficulty in reaching the Lake. When it came to a question of which one of them was to stay in comparative comfort with the prisoner-to-be, while the other dared the arctic rigors of Wickiup Flat, Jeb had no hesitation in choosing the post he preferred.

Kent was suddenly disturbed from his reveries by a whinny from Pedro. Looking up he saw two mounted figures just beyond the edge of the sheltering branches. Their noiseless advance through the snow had been unnoticed.

"Howdy," he called out cheerily. "Come right in, gentlemen . . . plenty of rooms to-day . . . American or European plan, as" . . . The facetious greeting died in his throat, with his first clear glimpse of the leading visitor's face.

"*Callier!*" Despite the disquieting fears which welled up within him as he recognized the sales manager, Kent contrived to keep himself well in hand.

"Howdy," said Callier, dryly. "Receivin' callers?"

Kent, still lying upon his blanket, his head and shoulders resting on the saddle, nodded as he met the sales manager's glance coolly.

"That being the case," said Callier, "I'll introduce our mutual friend, Jeb Watterson . . . who's just now parading about these parts as a *deputy sheriff*."

As Callier spoke an inkling of their purpose dawned upon Kent. Instinctively he straightened up and was halfway upon his feet when the ditch rider's cold voice checked him.

"No, you *don't!*" The speaker's hitherto hidden hand had emerged from his mackinaw pocket holding an efficient looking revolver steadily on the young man.

Kent subsided. He realized he might as well take whatever was coming calmly.

"That's bad medicine, Callier," he remarked quietly, "threatening a law-abiding citizen with a gun" . . .

"Law-abiding hell! At present writing you ain't got no more rights than a rabbit. Has he, Jeb?" The deputy sheriff, who had tied the horses near Pedro, now stood beside Callier, his ruddy open countenance in marked contrast with the shifty cunning of the other. He grinned assent.

"What's the point?" Kent persisted.

"Tell him," said Callier.

"Duty is duty," sighed Jeb, extracting a warrant from his vest. "David Kent, you're under arrest" . . . The official pronouncement was delivered with commendable gruffness, but the subsequent remarks seemed unprofessionally cordial if not actually apologetic. "And say, Dave, there ain't no use making any fuss. Just surrender peaceable and decent-like. This here warrant's all hunky dory and there ain't no way in the world of beating it . . . leastwise there ain't," he added with a memory of bygone legal maneuvers, "till you get to one of them lawyer guys."

"But Jeb, what am I being arrested for?" and as an afterthought, Kent added, "and what's Brother Callier's place in the party . . . surely I'm not such a desperate bird it takes two of you to cage me?"

"I don't mind answering that myself," put in Callier. It was evident from his tone that he not only did not mind, but actually enjoyed the opportunity. "You're arrested for destroying other people's property, and probably there'll be a charge of burglary or housebreakin' waiting when you get back." . . .

"But whose property?" interjected Kent.

"Why, the *Pioneer's* . . . Pharaoh Jones's, that is . . . you're the one that broke into his shop last night and smashed up a whole lot of newspaper stuff."

"But, man, the *Pioneer* doesn't be—" . . . Kent's mouth hung open on the incompleted word, and he became abruptly silent.

"I suppose my precious friend Failing cooked up this little scheme," he continued. "That explains your presence."

Callier grinned. "Oh, no," he said, "I'm only assisting Jeb. Knowing it'd be such a plumb lovely day up here on Wickiup Flat I just couldn't help coming along." He stopped to arrange a new chew of tobacco, enjoying Kent's suspense. "But my real job is over at Lost Lake" . . . Despite the fact that he had seen what was coming, Kent's face became perceptibly tense. "Ever been there, Mr. Kent?"

Just at that minute the young man's greatest ambition was to choke the sales manager. Unable to gratify it, he concentrated upon his effort to look unconcerned, and said nothing.

"Well," drawled Callier, "I thought you had. It's a plumb beautiful lake with plenty of water. You can't have irrigation without water, can you, Mr. Kent?" He was fairly purring now.

Again his only reply was silence.

"And it's a freakish bit of water, that," drawled on Callier. "I'm told you can tip it either way." He chewed his cud reflectively. "Well, I must be going now. Jeb here'll look after you till I get back."

Dropping the revolver in his pocket, Callier climbed on his horse. "And say, *Mister* Kent, just a leetle word of advice from a tinhorn gambler . . . Remember how you called me a tinhorn, *Mister* Kent? . . . When you've got a good hand don't never go and tell no one about it until the bets are made . . . especially a woman!"

And with that the sharp-faced sales manager started westerly in the teeth of the storm.

"The dirty skunk!"

"Uh-uh." Jed's comment on this characteri-

The Brain Storm 239

zation of Callier could be interpreted as either negative or affirmative.

But Kent was too busy with his own thoughts to notice whether or not the deputy agreed with him. The ditch rider's parting shot had hit home . . . not a straight, manly blow, to be sure, but a foul below the belt, which hurt all the more because it came unexpectedly.

"*When you've got a good hand never tell about it until the bets are made.*"

What did Callier mean? When had he heard that advice before? It sounded oddly familiar . . . Then it came to him; there flashed back into his mind his talk with Valentine . . . *he himself* had said almost those very words when the girl had asked why he did not at once tell her father of the Lost Lake plan.

"*Especially to a woman!*"

Callier, with his ugly sneer, had said that, too—and what his insinuation meant was as clear as the driven snow. Callier was as good as telling him that the woman to whom he had shown his hand had tipped him off . . . that Valentine Pennoyer had betrayed his confidence, abjectly. That was all he comprehended, all that mattered, as he laid his head on his arm there upon the cold ground. For the minute all the warm courage and resolve ran out of him. He felt unutterably broken and actually physically sick, with that sudden numbness at the pit of the stomach which many a brave man has known. It was the girl who mattered most, and what the girl had done. Nothing else counted; it was all a weary waste of effort.

"Never mind, lad, it's not so bad. Them lawyer fellers'll get you out of it all right." Jeb misinterpreting Kent's collapse tried to cheer him.

The deputy was easygoing kindness personified, with a disposition of almost childish trustfulness which saw the duty immediately before it but little else. Persistency was his besetting virtue, a very real one in a deputy whose occasional avocation is man-chasing.

"Oh, I'm not worrying about your damn warrant," Kent growled testily, pulling himself together. "That's the least of my troubles."

"Uh-uh?" That sounded curious to Jeb. A glimmering suspicion that perhaps his quarry was "wanted" for a bigger crime than simply destroying property filtered through his mind. He grasped his revolver more firmly.

"Say, Jeb," he raised himself on his elbow, one hand beneath him, "where's Cal . . ."

He stopped in astonishment, looking into the muzzle of the deputy's weapon.

"Now let's see that other hand" . . . the cautious Jeb admonished . . . "so . . . that's better. And just keep 'em both in sight, please."

Kent's sense of humor was stronger than his impulse to be angry. It was the second time in his life he had intimately viewed the business end of a revolver.

"Gosh!" he sighed resignedly, "there's more guns out in this blizzard than I ever saw before. Now look here, Jeb, I don't like you to point that cannon at me. It doesn't seem . . . well, exactly friendly."

The conversation was a bit confusing, but Jeb remained unrelenting. "Gotagun?"

"Good Lord, no! I never carried one in my life. Just take a look and see for yourself." Kent held his hands aloft while Jeb cautiously poked his pockets and other likely abiding places of a six shooter.

Much relieved, Jeb stepped back.

"Say, looky here, Dave, I've a proposish for you. I don't want ter be sittin' up here coverin' you like a hoss thief an' I reckon it tain't needed, but in course I can't take no chances. But if you'll give me your word you won't try to get away it'll be all right with me . . . your sayso's good here."

"That's sensible, Jeb. Of course I'll give you my word . . . I promise not to try to get away so long as you're with me."

"An' you won't try to get my gun?"

To that Kent also agreed, so prisoner and jailer speedily established an *entente cordial* under whose beneficent influence Jeb's holster, with its gun, was hung on a knot against the fir tree's trunk while its proprietor replenished the wood supply.

"And now tell me where Callier has gone?"

Watterson complied, recounting all he knew of Callier's plans to file on Lost Lake. Kent took the news quietly. He had already anticipated the plans of his adversaries, and what made his blood boil was the realization of how well they were working out.

He seemed so helpless, so well beaten. And he hated to be beaten! He had determined to win. Was there no way out of it? Again and again he asked himself that question, and could find no answer. Could he but reach Lost Lake ahead of Callier!

"If I could only post the notice there'd be some chance of beating them out at Farewell," he said to himself. "At least I could give bail and get down to Salem at the same time Callier did. There I'd have the same chance as he, and perhaps a better one when they heard my story."

But why waste energy in hopeless wishing? He was a prisoner, guarded by a friendly jailer to whom he had given his word not to try to escape. He felt certain, without testing the question, that honest Jeb could not be bought off . . . he might be circumvented, but never purchased. And Kent, pondering the problem, cursed himself for having promised anything; at least it would have been worth while, and rather exhilarating at that, to have tried physical conclusion with the deputy.

Round and round the hopeless circle Kent's thoughts wandered, while he cuddled close to the fire and damned the driving snow which had brought on all this trouble. Then suddenly an idea struck him, and he sat very still for many minutes, working out its details.

Jeb smoked complacently at the other side of the fire. Noting his companion's long silence, he offered something jocular about not getting the blues. But instead of answering, Kent's teeth began to chatter, and the more he apparently tried to control them the more they shook, until his whole body seemed gripped with ague.

Kent pointed at his head. Finally he managed to gasp, "It hurts . . . my God, how it hurts!" Then the paroxysm passed, and the sufferer quieted and for a time remained rigid and motionless, his eyes closed and his lips convulsively forming unspoken words.

Jeb was genuinely disturbed. He didn't know what to make of it or what to do. Then Kent seemed to regain control of himself. His lips were still. His eyes again opened, groping about with a puzzled look. Meeting the troubled gaze of the good-hearted deputy they all at once cleared up as if full understanding had returned to the brain behind them.

"Oh, Jeb" . . . the voice was shaken, apologetic . . . "I'm so sorry . . . so ashamed. You see, these" . . . but Kent's feelings overcame him, and burying his head in his hands his body shook with sobs.

"Now, now, Lad, take it easy," counseled Jeb gently, patting the shaking shoulder. "S'all right . . . everything's all right."

Bravely the young man nodded, wiping away the tears as he raised his head.

"It's good of you, Jeb . . . good of you." Just what was good of him Jeb didn't know, but he felt appreciative. "You see, Jeb, it's just this I feared . . . it's an old weakness. I . . . that is" . . . he hesitated, as if ashamed to make the disclosure, then, seemingly realizing the necessity of it, plunged on gulpingly. "It's up here, Jeb, old friend." He tapped his forehead. "Ever since I had typhoid they come on me . . . especially when I'm played out. And I suppose it's being up and riding all night with nothing to eat, the cold . . . and . . . and the excitement and the storm and all that which has brought it on now . . . Oh, God!"

Jeb's arm steadied him as he swayed, moaning.

"Yes, it's *them*, all right . . . the second one's due now any minute."

"Fits?" The deputy had a profound horror of mental derangement. He positively feared the insane.

"About the same thing," Kent assured him wanly. "Sort of temporary insanity. Only lasts half an hour or so but it's awful while it's on. Head feels all red hot . . . Listen, Jeb." He grabbed his companion's horny hand in his, and the deputy could have sworn that hand was fever-hot already. "I just hate to make such a mess of things but you've got to know about it—know what to do."

"Do? Me do?" Jeb's echo was weak. Kent raced on in a burning disquieting whisper.

"Yes. Pretty soon now I'll go entirely off my head. It won't last long but it's fierce while the spell's on me. And . . . and . . . Jeb, I'm awfully dangerous, they tell me . . . For God's sake keep that gun away . . . don't let me see it . . . don't you dare touch it. . . . There's just one way to handle me, the doctors say" . . . he gasped for breath. Clearly the fit was hard upon him.

"Yes, yes," Jeb, bending over him, was all anxious eagerness.

"It's just to humor me . . . don't forget that. . . . I'm likely to do anything and want anything . . . and let me do just what I want to . . . don't argue . . . don't try to stop me. Once" . . . Kent gasped for breath . . . "once when I had one of 'em at a hospital and wanted to get out of bed a fool nurse . . . a man, too . . . tried to stop me" . . . there ensued a palpitating silence . . . "the . . . poor . . . fellow . . . didn't . . . recover . . . for a month . . . it was awful the way I . . . mangled him."

The last words came out jerkingly. Then all at once the stricken one screamed in anguish and clapping both hands to his head doubled up upon the ground, rolling about wildly and moaning like a Beduin.

The details of those early spasms need not be recorded. Suffice to say that shortly they wore off, ushering in the third and most trying stage of the paroxysm.

In this Kent regained the use of his limbs. His eyes apparently could see, but they were strangely fixed and glassy. He moved and looked and even spoke like a sleep-walker, or, say, a madman in a play. Whatever the style, it was terribly disconcerting to Jeb, who stayed safely out of reach, always contriving to keep the fire between himself and his demented prisoner, and devoutly hoping the convulsion would end speedily. He didn't in the least fancy being left alone there in the wilderness with this epileptic maniac and cursed his luck heartily because he had not gone to the lake and left Callier with Kent. And the thought of Callier out there in the blizzard made his heart sink . . . suppose this lunatic should take the notion to decamp? What could he do? However could he hope to control or stop him? . . . He soberly recollected the fate of that nurse who had crossed Kent . . . supposing the madman attacked him, perhaps killed him, and then wandered away to be lost and die in the storm? Jeb's slow-going mind, once unloosed, performed miracles of dismal foreboding.

But fortunately the afflicted young man seemed possessed with no homicidal intentions.

"Good old Jeb!" he muttered time and again, smiling sillily and apparently seeing nothing at all. "Good old Jeb . . . God bless'm."

Swaying, with arms stiffly outstretched before him, he moved to the tree where his saddle-bag hung and groped in it. Seemingly he found what he wanted, for all at once he commenced gibbering inanely—half whimpering . . . and when he turned Jeb's heart sank in his boots, for the poor fellow's mouth was now foaming and frothy.

Still, however, he was safe. At least, Kent paid no attention to him. His one thought seemed to be the package he had taken from the saddle bag. This he hugged ardently in his arms, crooning a gibbering lullaby with his horrible frothing lips as he took it back to the fire and sank to the ground, cross legged. Slowly, carefully, tenderly he undid the fastenings.

Jeb's eyes followed every movement, wide and staring. But this apprehensive suspense was as nothing to the good deputy's consternation when the contents of that package were disclosed.

"Mother of God!" he ejaculated. "*It's dynamite!*"

Which it was—two gray soapy looking sticks, cased in their greasy skins of paper. Why Kent had brought them all that distance, safeguarded from explosive jolts solely by the extra flannel shirt in which the package had been tucked, only Kent, with his unspoken plans concerning the waters of Lost Lake, knew. And Kent, of course, was clear and clean out of his head, beyond the possibility of explanations immediate, or, should the dynamite explode, remote.

"*And* caps!" Jeb voiced his second observation in a horrified whisper.

For the insane young man also had in his hands

two copper firing caps, the little "ticklers" which are rammed down upon the sticks, causing the dynamite itself to detonate when the fire of the fuse reaches them.

Jeb's knees were actively clanking together by now. Pop-eyed, he watched the operations across the fire, like a bird charmed by a snake. Poor Jeb was hypnotized . . . hypnotized with fright. Cold perspiration, dripping down over his eyes, clouded the details of the impending tragedy.

And there sat the insane Kent, presumably in the midst of the final paroxysm of his horrible malady, gibbering vacantly and intently fastening a cap to one of the sticks.

"For the love of God!" The deputy's cry was anguished.

Kent's hands stopped. His lips ceased moving. For an instant he seemed frozen almost into consciousness, back to reason. Then a diabolical crafty smile distorted his face, with its slobbering mouth and froth-smeared chin.

"Ha, ha!" he cackled wildly, then tried to look across the fire at Jeb, but with foolish set eyes that seemed to see nothing, like a sodden drunken man endeavoring to appear soberly dignified. "Jeb, ol' frien', does dynamite freeze?"

Jeb's terror stricken lips could frame no answer.

"Br-r-r! It's bitter cold up here, Jeb ol' friend. I'm frozen . . . that's what makes my head hurt so. And if I'm frozen why" . . . the smile was sly with the logic of insanity . . . "of course the dynamite's frozen too. But it mustn't be frozen, Jeb, ol' friend . . . that wouldn't do at all. So what will David do?" . . . he was holding one stick in his hand now, fondling it like a doll and talking to it. And Jeb, to his infinite horror, saw that he had attached the firing cap which would explode the stick the moment it was struck or ignited. "So David will warm the poor lil' frozen stick. He'll just make a nice warm place here in the fire first."

With a bit of branch in his free hand the crazed man was patting out a resting place among the red coals.

Then he lifted the dynamite, leaning forward so as to place it in the fire where it would fall among the hottest embers . . . and Jeb waited to see no more. With a heartbreaking shriek he rushed to his horse, fortunately still saddled, and just as the explosion came, horse and rider crashed off through the low branches, the panic-stricken deputy yelling with horror.

When Jeb subsequently swore that he had heard the report of the explosion, occurring just as he swept from under the tree, he was adhering strictly to the truth. There was an explosion. It followed immediately the forward toss of Kent's hand. *But it was the explosion of a firing cap.*

Thrown in the edge of the embers furthest from him, the cap promptly went off with a startling report . . . enough, coupled with the violent departure of Jeb and the other horse, to frighten Pedro out of all sense of discipline; rearing back in terror he broke his tie rope and galloped off down the home trail.

Kent wiped the ashes from his eyes, blown there by the miniature explosion. Aside from further soiling his already soap lathered face no damage had been done.

"Well, I've lost my jailer," he said to himself. "If he'll only stay lost. It's no joke, though, about Pedro running off . . . perhaps he'll come back."

"Jeb can't say I didn't play square with him anyway." he addressed the fire argumentatively. "I promised I wouldn't run away or grab his gun and I didn't . . . He did the running away." He chuckled at the thought of the deputy's hasty decampment. "But if I loaf around here first thing I know brother Jeb'll be coming back to bury the pieces of his poor insane friend. Ugh! That soap tasted like the devil!" He wiped the suds from his face and removed the taste of his made-to-order froth from the inside of his mouth as best he could.

"We'll move now, horse or no horse. I'm going to get to that durned lake or know the reason why." And with that he started to replace the two sticks of dynamite in the shirt when a new idea suddenly struck him. After a momentary consideration he adopted it, chuckling delightedly.

"I hate to ruin the saddle, and it's a shame to

make Callier put on crepe . . . but the job may as well be finished right."

Quickly he imbedded another cap in one of the sticks of dynamite. Then from the saddle-bag he took out a small coil of fuse, from which he cut off three feet or so, fastening one end to the cap. Next he burrowed out with his feet and a stout stick a depression close beside the fire where he had been sitting and placing the dynamite stick at the bottom covered it over with as much dirt as he could scrape up, adding all available bits of branches and a few heavy stones. Lastly on top of all he rolled a sizable log, draped the saddle over it, and as a final detail hung Jeb's holster on the horn.

He fastened up the saddle-bags then, one containing the remaining stick of dynamite carefully wrapped in the flannel shirt, and arranged them over his shoulders, the straps across and around his neck and chest, the bags themselves hanging down his back.

"Here goes . . ." The match met the end of the fuse.

And as David Kent dodged off into the thicket, the flame licked briskly toward the buried dynamite, and then with a dull roar and a spout of dirt and debris came the explosion.

"*Requiat in pace* David Kent . . . esquire." Kent looked back at the smoking volcano beneath the tree, and hunching his burden into position trudged westerly out upon storm swept Wickiup Flat.

CHAPTER XXIV

LOST AND FOUND

An hour after he started out afoot in his desperate effort to reach Lost Lake, David Kent was hopelessly lost. Out in the midst of Wickiup Flat where already drifts were driving over the low landmarks and the snow came down so steadily that there was nothing to be seen but the blanket of white on the ground and the slanting flakes in the air, he ploughed forward steadily until somehow, despite the wind which should have been his guide, he became confused and lost.

Kent trudged along doggedly, all his senses alert to catch any sight or sound which might guide him. By now he was prodigiously tired and understood fully the gravity of his situation. He was genuinely lost, and to be lost in a snowstorm on this mountain plateau was serious business. And yet he could not comprehend how he had lost himself, for he had exercised every caution to keep the north wind coming directly on his right hand, feeling sure that by progressing westward he would soon strike the draw which lead to Lost Lake. But he had come more than the two miles that should have intervened, and there was no sign of any depression—only the everlasting gray expanse of the plain.

Finally the lost man stopped entirely. Unless the storm let up he saw no prospect of finding either the Lake or himself. And the storm did not abate, but instead its gusts swept down upon him with increasing rigor. He was near the point of exhaustion . . . the hard experiences of the last twenty-four hours had sapped his strength and the cold was finishing the work. His mind felt utterly weary . . . determination and combative power were at a low ebb. It was all he could do to resist the impulse to throw away the saddle-bags and sink down in the snow for a rest . . . a rest . . . yes, that was what he craved . . . if he could only rest . . . could escape this damnable snow . . . if he could only see something—anything but the everlasting gray driving flakes. He felt himself slipping . . . losing his grip . . . and dumbly he realized the danger of surrender. He must keep a stiff upper lip.

"Don't lose your head, lad," he whispered to himself.

And with a supreme mental effort, which seemed positively to wrack him, he pulled himself together and took stock of the situation. Clearly, the only sensible thing was to try to get back to the timber. He knew that his back track would be swallowed up in the snow, but with the wind for a guide at least he could find the trees somewhere at the fringe of the Flat, and thence there would be some hope of regaining the trail or even encountering Callier or the deputy. To stay where he was, or persist in the ill-fated effort to reach the lake, was simply to court disaster. He was beaten. That was clear.

So he turned back. As he did so his eyes detected an irregularity in the snow a dozen feet away, a little rough place just in the lee of a rounded drift, from whose top extended a bit of stick, weather-beaten almost as white as the surrounding snow itself. It struck him as curiously inexplicable, unless some animal had made it. With dull curiosity he stumbled over to the spot.

For an instant Kent gazed down dully upon that patch of roughened snow. Then all at once he fell to his knees, better to see the exact nature of the track. And track it was . . . the unmistakable imprint of a horse's hoof, pointing to his left, showed clearly. Apparently it had been kept uncovered through some freak of the wind which syphoned down over the steep little drift keeping almost clear a space just in its lee.

"It's a fresh track — made since the snow started," he argued to himself.

But whose track? And whither headed? Could it possibly be Callier's? If so, his heart sank realizing how hopelessly he was confused, for according to his calculations that track was headed south, while in reality, if it were Callier's, it should have been proceeding west. Then it occurred to him that perhaps it was the ditch rider's horse *returning* from the Lake. But that only made matters worse. Clearly, the wind had played some devilish trick upon him and he was irretrievably lost. Until the snow lifted, it was useless to try to make his way back to the timber . . . Heaven only knew where even the timber was . . . where the east lay he had no notion . . . it was all a ghastly tangle.

"Why, oh why didn't I bring a compass?"

He was at the very end of his tether. There seemed nothing to do but wait where he was . . . and ultimately freeze, he thought bitterly. No, he would not give up so easily . . . he'd fight it to a finish . . . at least he could try to make a fire. There must be enough shelter to shield a fire somewhere at hand. But wood? There were plenty of bushes out upon the Flat, he remembered, and occasional fallen trees, too, which had given up the hard contest with the elements. During the previous hour he had seen bits of branches sticking up through the snow and once had even stumbled over a log hidden under the white fall. He would find some wood. How good it would be to get really warm and cheat the bitter wind for a time!

Directly before him, sticking from the top of the neighbor drift, was a gnarled bit of whitened branch. That would make capital fuel, he thought, stepping forward to grasp it. But his outstretching hand stopped in mid-air, a sudden puzzling memory surging up in his brain . . . that weather-beaten stick looked strangely familiar . . . when had he seen it before?

Subconsciously he wondered if this was an hallucination, some ugly mental symptom of collapse . . . a sort of snow-bound mirage tricked into being by his weary brain.

Then abruptly his mind responded and he recollected with steel-cut clarity just when and where he had last seen that stick. Even Dad Trumble's words came back to him: "In Noo York I reckon they label the bygod streets, don't they?"

Feverishly he scraped away the snow at the base of the whitened branch. Sure enough, it was wedged between the topmost rocks of the monument which Dad had repaired and reinforced with this selfsame guiding branch as they had loitered there in August, looking down upon Lost Lake.

Kent gave a yell with all the strength of his lungs. And then another, venting his reaction from the despair of the preceding moment.

CHAPTER XXV

"ONLY A DRAW"

"WELL," said Dad glumly, "I reckon we're euchered."

Instead of answering the girl sat silently beside the fire, her eyes looking far along the trail which Callier had followed, seeing little of the surroundings, whatever mental panoramas may have unfolded before them. It was snowing so lightly now that one could see from the tamarack grove almost to the far end of the Lake where the trail mounted. There the edge of the storm still raging on Wickiup Flat lapped over into the hollow and its ragged flurries blotted out the figure of the departing horseman.

"Euchered . . . and a bygod snake-in-the-grass done it!"

"I'm sorry," the girl roused herself. She looked abjectly tired, but a reviving flush kindled her cheeks. "It looks as if we've been cleaned. But Dad, *it's only a draw.*"

"Eh?" The old man was at sea.

"David held the cards the first game . . . when he put Failing's special edition out of business . . .

score one for him. Then the others had a run of luck and side-tracked him with this arresting business . . . score one for them. That's a draw, isn't it? And now, Dad, we'll *play the rubber!*"

"An' the deck's stacked agin us." Despite his grumbling tone Dad felt the breath of renewed hope. "Got a card up yer sleeve, Honey?"

"An ace, Dad."

With that she bombarded him with inquiries about the Ringo Trail across the mountains.

"Will it be storming over there?"

"No. What's been snow here probably was rain there . . . and from the looks of it even the snow's due to stop soon. Leastwise, the snow hasn't reached down the west side more than a few miles . . . below it's probably purty as a picture."

"If one started out in a hurry, how long would it take to reach the railroad?"

Then Dad, whose mind was not agile in foresight, for the first time gathered what was coming.

"I'll be teetotally goswhizzled!" The old man considered the possibilities. "Well," he continued, after deliberation, "it's only a matter of six or seven miles down to the ranger station at Little Meadow. I could get there to-night . . ."

"But Dad, you haven't caught the idea. *You* aren't going at all!"

The girl returned his bewildered look with a confident smile.

"*I'm* the one who is going," she announced

calmly. "What's more, by the time our friend Callier reaches Salem there'll be dust on my filing for the waters of Lost Lake."

"Lord, child, don't talk such nonsense. It's . . . why, it just ain't *right* for you to be thinking no such thing. That's no trip for a girl to make by herself at any time, let alone starting out in a snowstorm."

"But Dad, you'll admit I could beat him to Salem."

"Prob'ly you'd get there first if you ever got there at all. But it's all plumb foolishness for you to go instead of me. Why shouldn't I go . . . ?"

"And leave me to find my way back to Farewell? No . . . unless I'm mistaken, it will be a harder trip home from here than it would be over to Salem. And besides, Callier knows you're up here and he doesn't know I am. If you are in Farewell to-morrow they'll never dream about the need of hurrying with their filing, and besides, you can tell David what's happening."

Finally Dad gave up. Crete was adamant; she had decided to go, and go she would. But another reason for the old man's silence was that he, too, had made a decision, namely to accompany the girl on the over-mountain trip, whether she wished it or not.

"It's clearing," Dad announced, "an' what's not so good, it's most three o'clock already. We . . . that is, you'll . . . have to hustle to reach Little Meadow before dark. Glad I got my Gov'ment key—it'll open the padlock down ter the ranger station."

"Better let me have it," she relieved him of the key. "Now, Dad, you get the saddles on and I'll run down and post my filing notice. Then will you ride along to the end of the canyon and tell me about how I'm to find the way?"

"Sure," he growled, adding under his breath, "and a heap farther, too."

When she came back from the Lake, having posted her notice on a tree near the one used by Callier, the horses were ready. Dad soused an armful of snow over the fire embers, and they mounted and turned toward the west.

For an instant they halted by the border of the Lake, the horses sniffing doubtfully at the unbroken snow lying over this new way they were being forced to follow, instead of the home trail.

Crete's gaze shifted from the flat white expanse to the dark rushing waters of the outlet creek . . . *hers!* A tingle of satisfaction warmed her . . . she had come to help David win the right to use that water, and now, forsooth, she was acquiring that right herself! Already she felt the pride of ownership in that snow-bound expanse.

Then he turned his horse into the knee-deep, virgin snow. Just as she prepared to follow a faint sound bore down to her, carried from afar by the lessening wind. She stopped in her tracks, listening intently. Then it came again, this time louder and more prolonged. First she thought it an echo of the storm, some wailing contortion of the wind. Next it seemed the cry of an animal, probably a discomforted coyote. All at once her straining ears caught the sound more fully. Unmistakably it was the call of a human!

"Dad! Oh, Dad!"

She was poised on Fantan's back, her hand to her ear, straining to hear.

"Sure it wasn't jest the wind?"

"Positive . . . the second time it came quite distinctly—from over there." She pointed eastward, where the gray snow shroud still hung over the edge of Wickiup Flat.

And as they listened, the sound of a voice halloing came unmistakably to their ears. Then in a sudden lifting of the snow cloud beyond the eastern limits of the Lake, where the home rail mounted to the level of the Flat, they saw a dark object. It moved, came nearer, then stopped, and the halloo echoed again.

Madly they shouted and waved their arms. The figure seemed to see them; he lifted his arms as if to wave, and then all at once sank down in the snow.

Crete was there first. In an instant she was out of the saddle and Fantan stood, with the reins on the snow by his forefeet, curiously watching his mistress. Dad, too, observed, and as he saw the unreserved abandon of the girl, usually so coolly self-possessed, the sight of her bending over the prostrate figure and lifting David Kent's head in her arm impressed him far more than did David's plight or the mystery of his presence.

"Jumpin' jeminy!" he ejaculated to himself. "You never can tell."

Having voiced that unanswerable axiom he pretended to busy himself securing Fantan, who really did not need to be secured at all, as he had quite enough manners to stay just where he was, after the way of all good western horses. After a discreet interval Dad drew near.

Crete was sitting in the snow, still with David's head upon her lap, rubbing his hands briskly, and oblivious of everything but the tinge of color creeping back into his cheeks.

"Fainted?"

"Yes . . . exhaustion, I suppose. His pulse is picking up now."

"It'll pick up faster when he opens his eyes," he said, half-aloud.

"Ssh!" she cautioned, "he's coming to."

But despite the admonition Dad chuckled outright.

Then the eyes in the pale face flickered and opened. Wonderingly they looked up into the blue eyes just above them.

"Crete!" The girl's name came instantly to his lips, which smiled wanly.

The fire beneath the tamaracks was rekindled and under the invigorating influence of hot tea, bread, and jerky Kent's spirits rose rapidly.

Then, and not till then, they plied him with questions.

"Callier told Dad you were arrested. Now you tell us just how much he lied. What were you doing trapsing around afoot . . . where's your horse?"

"To be exact, Mr. Interlocutor," he replied to Crete's questions, "Callier didn't lie at all . . . there's an exception to every rule. I *was* arrested . . . only I didn't stay arrested!"

Then he told the whole story. When he recounted the incident of the dynamite and his sudden mental affliction his hearers laughed uproariously.

"Goshalmighty! I'd have liked to see Jeb fade away," Dad guffawed. "An' say, won't it be a bird of a yarn he'll tell to Callier! Jes imagine the trimmin's he'll put on it. Wonder if they'll carve a nice neat epigraph on th' tree afore they leave the remains and take the sad news back to Farewell."

While the old man was considering the manifold possibilities of the situation Crete's thoughts were busy with more practical problems. What next? Her eyes encountered the saddle-bags, which Kent had contrived to keep with him throughout his adventursome day.

"What is the dynamite for?"

"Oh, that's a plan I worked out when I was up here before."

"Then you didn't bring it just to make a grave for yourself?"

"Not primarily. But it did come in handy for that . . . and the thorough way the job was done must have impressed friend Jeb when he came back to pick up the pieces," explained Kent, laughing again. "But I've got an even better use for the second stick, in that bag there. I'm going to start the water of Lost Lake flowing in the right direction . . . which is east instead of west."

"Remember what you said about miracles . . . they're way out of date," she chided.

"This one will come off O. K. With just a bit of a jolt in the ribs the old Chief will put it over for me."

Then he pointed to the great rock slide which veritably overhung the canyon leading westerly. With the snow piled up upon it, it seemed more than ever poised ready to crash down into the little valley at its base.

"Don't you see what a shot of dynamite would do up there?"

It was evident enough that a charge, well placed, would disrupt the entire lower section of the slide from its perilous angle of rest. Crete nodded. "I see . . . it would choke the canyon."

"And much more," Kent added. "Enough rock to fill the Panama Canal will slide right down just below the foot of the Lake smothering the outlet, unless my calculations are away off. When that end of the Lake is dammed of course the water will back up until it finds another outlet. And that's easy . . . it'll only take a couple of feet rise before it spills over into the old river bed where it used to go before this underground outlet formed."

Without a reasonable doubt, it seemed to both of them, the plan would work.

"For the love of Mike let's get a move on," Dad terminated the discussion. "We'll have to hurry to do this little engineering stunt of Dave's afore it gets dark. Anyway, she's mostly stopped snowing out on the Flat and it won't be hard to get home."

The plan was to block the Lake's outlet, after which they would hurry back to Farewell as quickly as possible. Crete, however, would slip into town alone, and as her presence on the trip to the Lake was unknown, she would be able to go on down to Salem, at worst together with Callier and at best perhaps ahead of him. Kent was to surrender himself immediately. Once Callier had him in custody, they agreed, he might delay the trip to Salem realizing that Kent could not get there first. And as a trump card, both Kent and Crete posted separate filing notices, not at the west outlet of the Lake, but at the east end beside the dry streambed. In each notice, and the copies of it, they specified clearly that they were filing on the outlet water of Lost Lake which *flows east*. Callier's posting, on the tree beside the existing outlet, was, of course, for water flowing "in a westerly direction."

"If it comes to a showdown at Salem," said

Kent to Crete, "and you and Callier try to file at the same time, they'll have to accept both filings pending an investigation to find out how this bally water really does flow . . . and when the engineers come up here next spring, Failing and his man Friday will throw a fit on the grass when they discover what's happened."

"An' I" . . . added Dad with devout profanity . . . "damwell 'd like to be in these parts when the glad news soaks in on 'em . . . I'd enjoy that 'bout as much as hearing Jeb tell about Dave's sewercide."

Draping his saddle-bags over his shoulder, Kent started along the westerly trail leading from the Lake's outlet down the canyon just below the overhanging rock slide. He meant to work around to the west side of the slide and then climb up it a couple of hundred yards to a point where a wart of giant bowlders projected out from the steep slope. A shot beneath them would start a general upheaval.

While the amateur dynamiter made the detour and worked his way up the difficult slope, crawling and slipping over the snow-covered rocks, Crete and Dad, with the horses, waited at the lakeside where the dark waters of the outlet stream gurgled. Their man-made avalanche, they believed, would bury that stream beneath countless tons of rock, shale, and earth.

The two watchers saw Kent work around the sides of great rocks which he could not clamber over. Now and then he slipped, in crossing steep-angled slopes, or sank suddenly when what seemed a solid surface proved soft snow drifted in between bowlders. But little by little he progressed toward the vantage point, always nursing his precious saddle-bags.

Suddenly for the second time that day, there came to their ears a distant cry.

"Quick, Dad . . . see who it is."

In an instant Trumble was back at her side.

"It's Callier and Jeb. They're coming this way."

The girl thought fast. Probably they had learned the truth about Kent's dynamite fake, and certainly if they found him, he would be re-arrested. And if she were discovered too, it would ruin any chance she might have of beating them to Salem for the filing.

"Dad . . . you go back to them . . . keep them from coming this way if you can . . . try to get rid of them . . . I'm going to dodge down the canyon and warn David."

Not waiting for a reply, she urged Fantan through the snow where Kent's foot tracks showed.

Dad swung his horse easterly, and trotted out along the Lake to meet the newcomers.

Jeb could scarcely wait to reach him, calling out when a hundred yards away, "Seen Kent?"

"Eh? What's that?" Dad wanted to get information, not to give it. To the question, repeated by Jeb and Callier in unison, the old man shook his head.

"Hardly. How could I see him when you folks got him arrested?"

Callier looked at Jeb and the deputy looked back at him. The features of both were troubled, and their eyes wandered furtively.

"What's wrong, gents . . . if I might ask? You-all seem consid'ble discombobbled, so ter speak."

Callier nodded to the deputy, as much as to say, "You tell it." And Jeb licked his lips.

"That Kent" . . . he began, shakingly . . . "he's gone and killed himself."

"My God!" The horror of the tragedy was echoed copiously in the old man's exclamation. "Killed? . . . Man, you don't mean to say as David Kent . . . my good friend Dave . . . has killed himself?"

Then a swift glint of suspicion seemed to penetrate the brain of this good friend of David Kent. With a cold, keen glance frightfully unpleasant to Jeb, he regarded the deputy.

"You say as how he killed *himself?*"

There was no doubting the implication of that emphasis. Then Callier came to the rescue of the floundering Jeb.

"That's just it, Trumble. Watterson was looking after the young fellow back there on the far edge of the Flat, under a tree out of the snow, where I left 'em to come up here. . . ."

"Ah! Then he warn't arrested at Farewell? . . . as you told me." There was an accusing tone to the old man's words.

"No . . . I stretched it a bit there. . . ."

"Um . . . stretched it, eh? Well, go on . . . let's hear it all."

Then Callier had Jeb disclose the details of the tragedy, which he did in faithful detail.

"So he went plumb crazy and fired the dynamite?" Dad asked in a subdued voice.

"He did. We've been back and there's nothing but a hole in the ground where we sat . . . even the saddle's blown to bits. My God!" . . . the poor man put his hands over his eyes as if to shut out the tragic picture . . . " to think how near it come to ketching me!"

The thought of that narrow escape seemed to unnerve Dad, too. Tears stood in his eyes . . . at least, they were wet . . . as he laid his hand upon the deputy's shoulder and said in a shaking voice, "Praise be, you got off, anyway . . . An' Jeb, man, don't take it so to heart."

"Now," put in Callier, none too steady himself . . . "we've come to get you to go back with us . . . sort of want you to look it all over . . . the place where it happened, you know . . . so as . . ."

"Yeh, I see. Want me for a witness . . . sort of to explain matters . . . corrobber you two, so ter speak."

"Jusit." Jeb, jabbing at his eyes with the

back of his hand, seemed relieved. "There might be . . . well, some folks might sort of try to talk ugly. . . ."

"They might," Dad agreed dryly.

"Look here" . . . Callier's manner was suddenly suspicious . . . "What's all these?" He pointed to the horse's tracks along the trail on which Dad had just ridden up to them.

"What, them? Why, them's horse tracks," replied Dad, his blue eyes widening with honest candor.

"Hell, yes . . . but whose horse? There's been more than one critter over here."

"Yes . . . an' no, Mister Callier. There's only been one horse, so far as I know, which is mine . . . but we've been up and down here a couple of times."

"And what you been doing waltzing back and forth?"

"Wall, as I reckon you've guessed already there ain't no harm in telling you. You see, I was planning to work out a leetle power development scheme . . . for some friends of mine . . . they jest wrote for me to get busy . . ." he rambled on, seeking fresh fictional inspiration as he progressed. "So I been getting the measurements they wanted . . . and it's kept me moving about considerable. See?" The guileless eyes regarded the sales manager hopefully. "And now, gents, let's be going . . . if we don't move it'll be dark afore we get to where poor old David . . . was killed."

But instead of acting on his suggestion, Callier was off his horse and studying the tracks in the snow.

"Not so fast, my friend," said he. "I'm no tracker, by a long shot, but unless you shifted the shoes on your horse there's something here I don't sabe." He had discovered that two sets of hoofs showed going westward, but only one returned. Just at that place the footmarks left by Kent did not show, as Fantan had followed them closely, scuffling up enough snow to hide any trace except to a more experienced eye than Callier's.

The sales manager mounted his horse, then, and started back along the tracks toward the outlet. "I'll take a look for myself," he said. And as there was nothing else to do, Dad followed, swearing fluently under his breath and wondering what would be the next turn of this eventful day.

They came to where Dad and Crete had waited, watching the dynamiter. Casting a furtive glance up to the rock slide, the old man was relieved to find that Kent was just then hidden. But if Callier could not see his ex-prisoner, and as yet entertained no suspicion that he and the deputy had been duped, he could see the horse tracks which continued along the canyon westward. Dad's eyes, better trained, also saw a footmark, clear cut in the snow, where Fantan's hoofs had failed to cover Kent's track.

"Whoa! Goldern ye, whoa!"

Callier turned, attracted by the sudden uproar.

Unaccountably, Dad's horse, until now a beast of model deportment, became momentarily unmanageable. He reared and swung around, the rider tugging at the reins and profanely urging him to be quiet. Before he gained control, however, the fractious animal had stamped the clean snow into a mass of hoofmarks. It happened, too, that the tell-tale footprint was completely obliterated. Then the horse quieted down as suddenly as he had commenced his antics, wondering, probably, why his usually considerate rider had raked his ribs so strenuously with the foot furthest from Callier.

The sales manager glared with growing suspicion. There was something wrong, but just what he didn't know. His immediate problem was to discover that other horse and his rider.

"Who is it?" Callier was angry, and showed it.

"Search me." Dad's manner was frankness itself. "Suppose it might be a ranger . . ."

"Ranger, hell! You can come or stay, just as you like, but I'm going to find out who's been with you."

Callier turned to beckon Jeb, who had lagged behind them; and was just in time to see the disheartened deputy gazing open-mouthed, up the mountain. Callier followed the direction of Jeb's awe-struck gaze. And suddenly his own jaw fell.

A matter of three hundred yards up the steep slope, the dark figure of a man was outlined against the snow. He was stooping, at the base of a mass of rock which rose from the slope beside him. Then the figure straightened up . . . unmistakably it was Kent.

"Mother of God!" shrieked Jeb.

Callier was not so readily impressed by things supernatural. It was Kent alive, and not Kent's ghost which he saw and wanted.

"There'll be no slips this time . . . and no damfool suiciding," growled the sales manager, drawing his revolver.

CHAPTER XXVI

NATURE TAKES A HAND

As he arranged the dynamite, wedging it deep into a crevice at the base of the overhanging mass, Kent calculated he could readily cross the slide and be out of danger in the interval between firing the fuse and the actual explosion.

"David, . . . Oh, David!" Crete's voice carried up to him. Turning he saw the girl, who had scrambled up the slide.

"Quick!" she called, "They're after you."

"Who?"

He guessed well enough.

"Hurry! Start the slide!" She was nearer now, panting with exertion.

"But how . . ."

"Listen to me." Her tone, breathless as it was, forbade argument. "Fire the dynamite and come down this way. . . ."

"But the slide . . . we can't get back" . . . he expostulated.

"We're not going back. . . . There they come now."

Kent, looking down toward the Lake, saw the

three riders at the foot of the eastern edge of the slide. As he spied them he himself was seen by the deputy and Callier.

Just as the latter raised his gun the young man ducked behind the rocks. The next instant the fuse was sputtering industriously, and Kent bounded off across the snow-covered slide to the west, with Crete racing before him.

The girl had reached the foot of the slope when the explosion came. Kent fared less well. A mighty gust of gravel and splintered rock shot into the air, spattering down all around him as he sped for safety. Just as he neared the foot of the final slope, a fragment of stone struck his head and he wilted in his tracks.

Crete saw him plunge into the snow where he lay very still. And she saw, too, on the slope above him, a portentious trembling. The main slide, started by the dynamite-loosened bowlders, in its initial rush had shaken and dislodged the masses to the east and west of it, and already the even white slope of snow was pitted by rolling stones and soiled where overhangs of shale and débris were shaking loose. The rumbling of the coming avalanche was in the air. And in the very path of the gathering danger lay the prostrate man.

Oblivious of the stones which already were hurtling down from the heights, Crete ran back. She scrambled up to where he lay, nearly at the base of the slope, his hair and the snow beneath it darkening with blood; and grasping his shoulders dragged him to the level. The slope was steep and his weight slipped readily through the snow. But once at the bottom, the difficulty of the girl's task doubled. First she tried to carry the body, but she lacked strength to get the weight upon her back, try as she would.

In desperation, she commenced dragging him through the snow. It was a bitterly hard task, but little by little she contrived to move the burden westward toward Fantan. Twenty yards she dragged him, and they were almost out of danger. It was heartbreakingly slow. Her breath came short from hot, hurting lungs, and perspiration dimmed her eyes. Struggling for fresh strength she looked up, and her face went as white as the face of Kent.

The slide had started. The upper portion of the talus slope quivered, poising in a last undulating shiver. The next instant, shrouded by a smoky cloud of dust and snow, the portion of the slope above thundered down toward them. The avalanche, Crete saw, reached to the very western edge of the talus.

With a cry of fear—fear not for herself but for the unconscious man—she resumed her task, her arms twined beneath Kent's shoulders. Stumbling, panting, half-fainting from exhaustion, she fought on with every atom of courage within her.

Just as Crete cleared the danger slope, the avalanche of rock and débris hurtled down, all frothy with dirty snow, engulfing the trail behind.

The dust of the great slide swept over them, and the cold breath of the air thrust asunder by the rushing mass chilled the girl's hot cheeks and fanned the clotted hair of the still man at her feet. It seemed the very breath of death—of death doubly cheated.

"Thank God! Oh, thank God!" cried out Crete Colton, sinking down beside the man she had saved.

Shortly the exhaustion of her overwhelming efforts wore off. And at once, as she regained her faculties she thought not of herself but of the injured man.

Taking off her heavy coat, the girl laid it on the ground beneath David while she examined the wound in his head. It had an ugly look—a long gash with bloody gaping lips—but it required no surgeon to see that it probably was at worst a deep scalp wound, accompanied, no doubt, by concussion.

Crete first opened her blouse and tore, with one whole-souled pull, the front portion out of the soft muslin chemise beneath, and with strips of this contrived a crude bandage. But the wound had bled profusely and before bandaging it was necessary to clear away the clotted mass of curly hair. There was no water, but she remembered the knife carried in the pocket of her divided skirt.

"Going to amputate?"

The words, whispered weakly, startled her almost into dropping the knife she was in the act of using. Twice that day David's eyes had opened upon this same fair-haired ministering angel bending over him. Only this time her face was averted at its task, and he had had opportunity to gather his senses and consider, in a dazed way, what had happened. Closing his eyes, after that first rift of recollection, a strange feeling of peaceful satisfaction came over him.

Then, looking again, he saw the knife and spoke:
"Going to amputate?"

The words, and the spirit of them, lifted her burden of fear. She had been bravely stoical while she worked, but the silence and the stillness of the man wracked her heart with foreboding.

"Yes . . . amputation's the only thing!" There was almost laughter in her words; the life in those brown eyes somehow brightened the whole world wonderfully. "Do you object if I perform it just above the shoulders?"

He contrived to smile, though it was a painful grimace.

"Go to it! My head hurts devilishly . . . feels 's if it had passed through a rock crusher . . . hack it off any way you please."

"No, I won't do that, either. To tell the truth" . . . the words trailed off into a whisper unheard by Kent . . . "I'm afraid I rather like it." Then, aloud: "But I am going to amputate some hair . . . it's the only way to clear away the muss . . . I'm afraid it will hurt."

With that she picked up tufts of the hair near

the wound and sawed them off with the knife, doing the best she could to make short work of the petty torture, while Kent gritted his teeth and inwardly prayed for a return of unconsciousness. When the girl wrapped her bandaging over the wound, however, she found the material too light and flimsy to stay in place, and to cure that she ripped a two-inch strip from her khaki skirt, with this stronger cloth binding the bandage securely in place.

"It looks like an East Indian headdress," said Crete surveying her work, "but at least it will keep your brains from leaking through."

"Ugh! I feel flabby, but that's fine . . . everything's fine now," said he, trying to be optimistic, but with his head swimming in circles.

"Oh, yes, everything is fine!" She repeated dryly. "Except of course that you've just escaped being killed by exactly one eighth of an inch and you're about as useful on a mountain trail as a mummy!"

"Well, get Dad and the horse and pack me home. Or turn me over to my late jailers and let them accept the responsibility," he suggested weakly.

"There isn't any Dad and there aren't any jailers . . . not on this side of the divide, David. Your blessed dynamite has fixed things so they won't be getting over for a good long time . . . or us back. You and I and Fantan are monarchs of all we survey." She looked around then, at the débris of the great slide, at the torn mountain side, and the white expanse to the west of them, hemmed in by cliffs.

"What do you mean?"

"Just what I said. We're babes in the woods . . . or boobs in the hills. The Ringo Trail has been blown to smithereens. Things happened just as you predicted . . . the Chief sloughed off a whole shoulder down upon what used to be the trail. It's absolutely choked up . . . there's no going back and no coming over."

They were silent then for a space. She, clear-headed, considered what was best to do, while the thought uppermost in Kent's clouded mind was realization that now at last all his Lost Lake hopes had gone glimmering.

"Well," said Crete, finally, "it'll be dusk soon. We'd better be going."

"Where?" The query came weakly. Kent cared little, just then, what happened to him. His head hurt abominably, his body ached, he was sick with utter weariness and this last discouragement had all but broken his spirit.

She told him of the ranger station Dad Trumble had said was six miles distant, and urged him to renewed fight. Buoyed up by the courageous hopefulness of the girl, Kent finally mustered enough strength to find his feet. His head swam, and one arm clung to Crete's shoulder while the other grasped the saddle, Fantan the meanwhile evidencing in every way possible his equine desire to be helpful.

At length Kent was in the saddle, where he clung giddily, and they moved off, Crete walking at Fantan's side, her arm steadying the uncertain rider. And frequently, during the long journey down the trail, first through snow, then beneath forests made doubly dark by the night, there was need of the girl's assistance. Time and again, were it not for the strong arm, Kent would have toppled off. Time and again, were it not for her cheery encouragement, he was ready to give up, craving nothing better than to lie where he might fall, and thereby alleviate the aching of head and body which even their careful gait made at times intolerable. But Crete would not listen to pleas for delay. She knew that if they rested once it would be doubly hard to go on again. And above all she feared that Kent might break down at any minute, and tried to forestall such a possibility by keeping on the move.

While she aided him, scolded him, cajoled him and, at times, actually supported him, the girl trudged along beside the horse, stumbling through the dark, tripping over roots and bruising her feet on unseen rocks. During the last half of that unforgetable journey she limped more than walked, and with her free hand hung heavily to the stirrup leather, seeking to lift some of the burden from her poor feet. Indeed, when they found the cabin, the girl was in little better shape than the man. Her physical strength about gone, she was sustained by pure nerve. But never a whimper escaped her, and her companion, wrapt in his own misery, guessed nothing of her suffering and the exhaustion against which she fought so bravely.

It was typical of western mountain ranger stations, that cabin. One small square room, with log walls and shake roof, was the beginning and the end of it, except for the overhung roof in front, extending in a sort of covered porch for fifteen feet and providing a shelter for stove wood, saddles, and the like. Surrounding the building, which stood in a patch of meadow land, was a neat fence fashioned from lodge pole pine, and various signs proclaimed Uncle Sam the owner and the serious inadvisability of interfering with government property.

Crete, however, had the Forestry Department key given her by Dad Trumble, and even before helping Kent to dismount she had opened the padlock and swung the door wide.

Aided by David's flashlight she found a candle and with its assistance was delighted to discover that the cabin appeared reasonably well stocked. A roll of blankets hung from a beam, and the bulk of a gunny sack, suspended nearby out of reach of rats, evidenced that at least some food was on hand. Beside the little rusty iron stove in the corner was a neat pile of split wood, and more, she noted, lay outside beneath the shelter roof.

"All ready to set up housekeeping!" she cried to David, emerging from her brief inspection.

"I'm all in." That was all he could say as he

sank into a chair fashioned from a packing case. And, in truth, he was. His last reserve of strength had ebbed away, and he sat there a listless wreck, his head buried in his hands and his body drooping.

Wasting no time on profitless compassion, the girl cut the rope holding the bedding to the rafter, and spread two of the four blankets upon the boards of the single bunk.

"Now, David!" She divested him of shoes and mackinaw, "Bed's ready."

With her arm about him, he stumbled to his feet and half-laid himself, and was half-laid, upon the waiting blankets.

Twenty minutes later two pots steamed on the stove. She propped him up then, and poured a taste of hot coffee into him, until, revived, he gladly swallowed the rest for himself.

"Ah!" he sighed sleepily, "that's the best thing of the day."

"Which isn't saying much, David, when you think what a day it's been. And now we'll try something which won't be so pleasant."

With that she brought the pan of hot water to the side of the bunk, and some strands of soft muslin which had been her own undergarments a few minutes since. As gently as could be, but painfully at that, the amateur nurse cut away the first bandages and with a soft bit of rag which had been boiled she bathed the scalp.

Holding the candle close then, she had her first good look at the wound for now that the hair was cut away and the blood cleansed it was possible to see its exact condition. The opening was perhaps three inches long, over the right ear. It commenced as a narrow cut at each end, widening at the middle into an ugly trough, perhaps a quarter of an inch deep extending down to the bone. The lips of flesh folded back as the leaves of a book, opened in the middle, turn back from the binding. Bleeding had nearly stopped, but during the hours since the accident the wound had stretched open, and apparently might widen farther if not checked.

Crete's choice lay in simply cleansing the wound and waiting for help, or in playing surgeon herself and closing it. Revolving the matter in her mind, she realized that medical assistance might be days in coming. So, tired as she was, she decided to do what seemed to her the safest thing then and there, if she could find something with which to work.

In ten minutes Crete had what she wanted. At least, she had promising substitutes. Providence had been kindly when it endowed the forest ranger who last occupied that cabin with housewifely habits. For her search revealed a couple of needles stuck into the log just beside the cracked mirror, and among the relics of a cigar box she unearthed a couple of casting flies fastened to a fine gut leader. Crete removed the flies, slit the top loop from the leader and ascertained that she could thread the gut through the eye of the larger needle.

Locating another candle she reinforced the single light, propping the two, each in the mouth of a bottle, just above Kent's head. That was the illumination of her operating-room. Then, with much water, freshly boiled, she cleaned her hands and arms scrupulously, and threaded up the needle with the leader gut, after first holding the needle itself in the fire flame to disinfect it. The gut she passed through the boiling water.

"It's the best I can do." She sighed to herself. "It will hurt, David" . . . her voice was steady enough as she explained her intention . . . "but remember, like the mother spanking the little boy" . . . she choked over her attempted laugh . . . "it will hurt me more than it does you."

It hurt, truly enough, but he bore it bravely, gripping the side of the bunk with his fingers and swearing deeply now and then as the needle pricked his scalp flesh and the catgut dragged through in its wake. It hurt her, too—every bit of it. But she neither spoke nor faltered. One, two, three, four stitches she took, forcing the needle through the protruding edges, pulling the gut after it and drawing the sides of the wound together as firmly as she could. And as she worked with her face hidden above his head, silent tears dropped down upon the curly brown hair and even upon the very wound itself. Perhaps it was those tears, she thought afterward, which disinfected so well and left no ill effects from the operation.

When it was over she gave her patient more hot

coffee, which was all he wanted, and wrapped him in the remaining blankets. The last candle was gone now, and she groped her way to the door, where the outer darkness showed less dark than the inner jet. Fantan, browsing in the grass, heard her and whinnied softly.

"Good night, pony."

She found the saddle blanket and with it turned to the cabin again. On the high threshold she paused, motionless for a moment. From the direction of the bunk came the sound of easy breathing, the even respiration of comfortable sleep.

"Thank God." She spoke very quietly, her whole soul in the words. Then she knelt upon the threshold log and the tears which flowed down her tired, stained face were tears of happiness, for Crete Colton, the schoolmistress whose acquaintance with good fortune had never ripened into intimacy, somehow found a joyful satisfaction in the peril, hardship, and sacrifice of this adventuresome day.

The tears were still undried when she lay down upon the saddle blanket, stretched on the floor opposite the bunk. For pillow she had one of her own saddle-bags, and for covering, her mackinaw and Kent's.

When David awoke and slowly became entirely conscious, the first dull light of dawn filtered through the open door and single window. Looking about he recalled the events of the preceding night, some of them seeming ages gone by, and others incidents scarcely completed. His hand went to his head, and he felt the bandages, just as his every sense could feel the inner soreness of the head itself and the bruised aching of various portions of his body.

"She actually sewed it up—God knows how!" He said it half-aloud. And lying there the wonder of the girl's courage bore in upon him, hazily like a good dream.

Thinking of her he all but dozed off again, until suddenly the thought struck home that something had happened to her—that she had left him. That waked him, clearheaded, though weaker than he knew.

He contrived to turn on his side, each movement rousing throbs of soreness throughout his body and pricks of pain in his head, and was on the point of calling aloud for Crete when his eyes saw in the semi-darkness on the floor a darker mass.

She lay against the opposite wall, as she had slept throughout the night. Her dusty hair had loosened and tumbled over the saddle-bag in towsled profusion. One arm was extended at length, the other lying across her breast, its hand clasping in place the mackinaw covering. He thought he could see, even through the gloom, a look of contentment upon her features, heavy as they were with sleep and exhaustion. The other coat, his own, which had been over the lower portion of her body, had slipped partially aside.

As he looked, full consciousness of his surroundings, and something more, surged up within him. He saw the girl stretched with so little to shield her from the hardness of the floor and the crisp chill of the night. He sensed the instinctive effort for protection and warmth in that arm across her breast, with its hand clasping the mackinaw. From that his eyes fell upon the two blankets so carefully tucked in over his own body, while his hands discovered two more were beneath him. And she had done that!

"You damn big cad!" he growled at himself.

He was wonderfully ashamed just then—a shame which actually made him quite sick and dizzy.

For a time he lay cursing himself wholesouledly. After a bit the resolve swept over him to reach out and take the girl's hand—that hand resting upon her breast, grasping the mackinaw—and kiss it. But before the notion took shape too definitely in his hot head, he saw its folly. Yes, he wanted to, truly enough . . . wanted to crush that hand and tell its owner oh, so many things; to lay all his gratitude at her feet . . . wanted to do all this, more, it seemed, than he had ever desired anything before.

Loosening one of the blankets from around him, he contrived to get from the bunk and lay it over the sleeping girl. It cost a supreme physical effort and sent him back in a spasm of dizziness. But it was worth the price, he thought. He did it with a queer sense of sacredness . . . he felt supremely decent.

Then he turned to the wall, and before sick-bed slumber banished the pains in his head and the aches in his heart David Kent rehearsed a number of good resolutions. And some of them he kept.

CHAPTER XXVII

AT THE RANGER'S CABIN

When David again opened his eyes he was alone, although the changed appearance of the surroundings testified someone's early morning industry.

The stove, rubbed into an approximation of brightness, radiated a cheerful warmth. A pot of coffee simmered, and in the open oven was visible the brown top of a pan of biscuits. The floor had been swept clean and a gay bunch of Indian paintbrush, arranged in a syrup can, decorated the decrepit table. Even the cracked mirror was resplendent, and the five-gallon gasolene tin, extemporized into a bucket, brimmed with clear water.

As the injured man noted these housewifely reforms their author entered. Her eyes were merry again, and her face glowed with color. The dusty hair, so abandoned when he last saw it, was now disciplined and piled in place.

"You look as fresh as a daisy." The hackneyed greeting seemed appropriate.

"Oh, I feel fine, thanks. I've just tried conclusions with a little creek at the foot of the meadow." She gave a mock shiver.

"Cold?"

"Greenland's tropical in comparison. Perhaps you don't remember everything that happened last night, but it's only about a mile on the back trail to snow. It's just as Dad Trumble predicted—snowing up there and rain down here. Only some of the snow has lingered in that water!"

It was, in truth, raining, in a gray persistent way typical of the western slopes of the Oregon Cascades. Now and then the grayness would gather blacker accompanying a brief downpour and then relapse into intermittent drizzling. Dampness dripped from the eaves and when occasional lazy breezes swayed the nearby trees the swish of dank foliage and spattering of dislodged water broke the sodden silence.

"No, I don't remember much about it," he admitted, adding to himself, "but there are some things I'll never forget."

"Well, how do you like my boarding house? And how is the star boarder himself?" she asked.

"Oh, it's a great place! Everything about it appeals to me, from the landlady to that coffee I see on the stove. . . ."

"You've got the order mixed!" she corrected, laughingly. "The coffee's by far the more important. It was a godsend. As a matter of fact, we're wonderfully lucky because there's about everything needed in the way of grub here, even down to baking powder. Witness" . . . she poked the pan in the oven out into full view . . . "they look edible, don't they?"

"Lord, yes! I'm feeling better already."

"Well enough to get up? How is the head?"

He twisted around a bit before answering, gingerly testing out the problem at first hand. The result wasn't altogether satisfactory.

"Taken all in all I'd say I feel like the end of a misspent life . . . but at that a hundred per cent. better than I did last night . . . thanks to you. And say," he hesitated, "did you . . . that is, I felt like an awful beast . . . after all you did for me . . . it . . . it . . ." He was floundering, but apparently the girl was too intent upon getting the biscuits out of the pan to notice. "Well, look here," he finally worked himself up into a similation of self-righteous anger, "it was positively wrong for me . . . that is, for you . . . oh, hang it! What I'm trying to say is I hope you didn't catch cold . . . it was a damn outrage for me to hog all the blankets."

As her back was toward him he could not see her face, which was just as well. To herself she said, "You didn't take the blankets, bless your heart." But at the same time she was thinking of the miracle whereby that blanket had found its way from his shoulders to hers.

"Do you think you can get up?" That was all she said aloud.

He thought he could.

At the Ranger's Cabin 293

"Well, then, you try it. Here are water and a basin. I'll be back in twelve minutes and we'll have breakfast."

With that she slipped on her mackinaw and went out into the soft drizzle. And in the appointed time she returned, bringing an armful of spruce boughs.

Kent, sore and shaky as he was, disposed of a goodly amount of cornmeal mush, coffee, and biscuits, and would have eaten more if Crete had permitted.

"It strikes me that for an invalid there's no end to your appetite," she remarked.

"Why should there be? I haven't had a thing to eat, except a couple of sandwiches, for thirty-six hours. I'm as empty as a vacuum cleaner, and it's working now you've turned it on!"

She noted that when the meal was over Kent was more than willing to get back to the bunk. He tried to make a show of being "all right" and taking a hand in the slight task of cleaning up the tin dishes, but his knees weren't steady beneath him and his head, he admitted regretfully, began to spin.

"What's the idea?"

Crete had brought in another armful of spruce boughs. He wondered what she meant to do, and asked. Indeed, he himself had no clear notion what should be done. He realized simply that for the time being he was down and out, with neither disposition nor ability to undertake anything beyond the confines of the bunk. And in this condition he felt immeasurably dependent upon the girl.

"The idea?" she repeated. "Why, I'm going to make you comfortable . . . unless you prefer bare boards to a nice mattress of boughs?"

"No indeed. But, Crete . . ." he hesitated, "I . . . that is, it would make me feel better if you'd take this bunk and . . . well, fix me up somewhere else . . . that is, if we have to stick around here. It's . . ."

"Yes, I know . . . it's embarrassing. That's what you started to say." She laid the boughs down and looked at him squarely, her level blue eyes frank and serious. "And from my standpoint, David, it could be even worse than that . . . no, don't interrupt! We've done the right thing and I've no regrets. But you know, and I know, that it might hurt both of us, hurt us in ways that can't be cured . . . if we stay up here for a day or a night longer than is absolutely necessary. Oh yes, that's true, and there's no harm in being sensible about it. That's why I'm going."

"Going?"

She had seated herself on the edge of the home-made "arm chair," facing him where he lay on the bunk. It was all thought out in her mind, and she was ready to discuss her conclusions frankly.

"Yes, I'm going. It's the best thing to do."

"How far is it?" He sighed. Those blankets seemed wonderfully comfortable and the thought of dragging himself along the trail, or being dragged on Fantan, was anything but inviting. "Do you think I can make it?"

"It's forty miles or so to the railroad, according to Dad. As for your second question, I don't think you can make it . . . and what's more, you're not going to try!"

She smiled broadly at his blank expression.

"You didn't understand. I'm going to leave you here. I hate to do it . . . more than you know." Her voice dropped. "But David, it's the only way. You couldn't possibly make the journey. With one of us walking it would take two days, and so far as I know there is no stopping place on the trail. However, if I ride I can push through quickly and then I'll send help back. That wound would simply open up and all sorts of complications might set in. But if you stay here and rest everything will come out finely and . . ."

"But couldn't you stay?" It was a small boy's plaint. After all, sick men and children are pretty much alike.

The blue eyes never wavered from his, but twice as she started to speak she seemingly changed her mind, and remained silent.

"I've told you, David"; finally she said, very quietly, "I'd do anything . . . *anything in the world*" . . . she choked a little there, and for the first time the blue eyes wavered . . . "for you. And David" . . . she was explaining like a mother now . . . "that wouldn't be best. I've . . . why, I've been trying to think about it from your standpoint, David. Don't you see? You and I are up here at this cabin and . . . and . . . oh, the only thing I can do is to go for help as soon as possible. *I don't mind for myself"* . . . the curious certainty of the words impressed her hearer . . . "but *she* would." She stopped then, tears very nearly in her eyes.

A growing wonderment filled him. Added to what he had already sensed himself, especially in that period of wakefulness at dawn, it sent a curious thrill throughout him, partly of bitter self-arraignment and partly the happiness of a new resolve. David Kent's mind and heart suddenly were wide awake.

"Valentine?"

Crete nodded.

"I don't see . . . what you mean," he lied. He did see, and he knew he saw. But on some inexplicable impulse he sought to drag it all out in torturing words. And Crete accepted the challenge, giving better than she took.

"You know your fiancée wouldn't like it . . . she'd never forgive you. She's angry enough already over your interference with her father's affairs, without risking anything more."

"But, Crete," he expostulated, "my Lost Lake plan has gone flooey . . . there's no more chance to make trouble for Father Pennoyer, worse luck! I haven't a thing to show for my pains but this

At the Ranger's Cabin

blame cut, and if it hadn't been for you I'd be neatly buried right now up there under the slide . . . a just reward, the Old Man would say, for messing in his affairs. And besides, you're talking like a prospectus of big business. It's unbecoming a lady and a settler."

The placid blue of Crete's eyes clouded. After all, she was only a girl who had been doing a hero's work. This bantering discussion of things which cut to her very heart was too much.

"Why, Little Girl," he swung out of the bunk as best he could, laying a hand on her shaking shoulder, "please, please don't. You've saved my life and you've nursed me like a sister and now you're . . ."

"I only want you to get what you want," she sobbed.

"And God knows I mean to get it." He was beside her now, his arm around her. Her head was bent low, and he kissed the dusty hair so softly she did not know it.

"Crete dear," he whispered, "don't you know what I want?"

As she felt him, then, beside her, his arm strongly holding her she cried softly and did not lift her head. And her heart ached more than ever before.

"Crete," he said again, gently urging her to look up at him, "what I want is *you*. I want you, dear, just *you*, more than all the world."

But still she was silent. Suddenly a new thought dawned upon him.

"Please, Crete, listen." He went back to the bunk then, sinking down upon it, too weak to stand. "I'm a rotter . . . God knows what you must think of me! Only . . . well, I'm going to show you I'm all right. It's . . . oh, I suppose it seems unspeakable to you to have a man you think is engaged turning right around and asking you to marry him. It looks rotten . . . I'm ashamed . . . ashamed of the looks of it, that is . . . the truth is all right and there's nothing that shouldn't be."

"You *are* engaged, aren't you?" The question came very softly.

"No, I'm not." Kent's own assurance surprised him. Not long ago he had considered, or, at worst, hoped himself engaged; latterly he had feared he was. "Val . . . Miss Pennoyer never promised me and . . ."

"But you promised her and you've been in love with her." The girl's words were not reproachful. It was a level statement of fact. Her good self-possession was regained.

"Look here, Crete," he tried to laugh. "I'll tell you the whole thing. You've been infernally square with me and I'll try to reciprocate. I *was* in love with Valentine . . . at least, I thought so, I'm not now . . . and I haven't been for a long time. I've blundered along, I'll admit, but I never really wanted her . . . only I was too much of a fool to know it or too big a coward to admit it. I did make a bargain with Valentine;

she put me on a sort of probation for a year and I haven't made good. . . . What's more, Crete, so far as that end of it is concerned, I don't care now whether I ever do, only . . . . well, the truth is I had set my heart on helping out with the settlers. That seems so awfully worth while."

"The Lost Lake plan came pretty near being killed off, didn't it?" she put in.

"Pretty near? Why, it is killed off—as dead as free silver." The thought deepened his gloom. "Thanks to you and Dad, though, it almost had a resurrection. You might have put it over if I hadn't reappeared on the scene and messed everything up with that dynamite and the slide—including my addle-brained head."

"You certainly came precious near addling it," she laughed. Evidence of downheartedness on his part seemed a sure signal for the return of her own good spirits.

"Crete, how did you get in on it?" He had become increasingly curious on that score as he pondered the events of the last day. "What brought you up into the hills?"

She regarded him quietly for a space, pondering some secret problem.

"You left a note in the safe, telling Pharaoh you were going," she said finally.

"But surely that didn't start you following me into the young blizzard." His interest was thoroughly aroused. "You must have known about the plan to arrest me."

She nodded, the color ebbing from her face.

"Come, tell me," he insisted, "it's puzzled me how those highwaymen got wind of it? So far as I remember Pharaoh and you and perhaps Dad are the only ones who knew about my plans with the Lake."

But scarcely were the words out of his mouth when he recalled, as vividly as if the conversation had just ended, his talk with Valentine on the porch of the Company House when he had unfolded all the chief details of his Lost Lake enterprise. What is more, the fact that he remembered, and guessed the truth, was written large upon his face. And the girl before him saw and understood, as thoroughly as if he had spoken aloud the bitter thoughts which crowded into his brain.

"*She* told them?"

Crete faced him steadily, in troubled silence.

"But why should she do it?" He was not completely bitter yet. That would come soon enough. Crete, with the in-seeing way of a woman understood that, too. And she felt curiously sorry for the other girl.

"It was her father you were fighting. What did you expect?"

"God knows!" he replied, letting his head fall back upon the blankets, so the throbbing would be gentler and he could, perhaps, think out some salvage from the wrecks about him.

Crete let him lie there while she worked. First she made dough, and after getting the fire in the

At the Ranger's Cabin 301

little stove on a substantial basis, where it neither threatened to burn out the oven nor leave its corners chilly, she set about baking as many biscuits as the available pans would hold. Also she found a sack of beans, and put a pot of them to boil. Then she filled the improvised water bucket and replenished the supply of firewood. Lastly she arranged the provisions where Kent could get them readily.

"Now, David, you'll have to try the chair again."

It was the first she had spoken in half an hour, and all the time he had been lying there with his face to the wall. When he had scrambled out she arranged the spruce boughs, which by now were dry, in the bunk, making a springy, sweet-smelling mattress. And upon it she permitted her invalid to climb, still glumly silent, after redressing his wound.

"Now," said Crete, "Fantan and I'll migrate. It's about noon, I imagine, although my watch gave up the ghost last night. I've arranged everything here so you will be comfortable and have plenty to eat. There's bread enough, of a sort, and if you'll keep sticking wood in the stove those beans will be edible by evening. And there's bacon, with a pan to fry it in, and all the corn meal you can eat, which only needs to be boiled. There's even sugar in that bag on the table. Altogether, you'll live like a king . . . and I hope you'll be comfortable."

She paused for a last look around. She was ready to go, and yet hesitated.

"Are you feeling all right? Is there anything else I can do?"

The words were woefully inadequate. They did not—they dared not—convey the emotion behind them.

"Crete," he roused himself, "you've made me so comfortable I'm positively ashamed . . . .except," he added ruefully, putting his hand to his head, "this head-piece of mine begins to waltz as soon as it's raised up a bit."

"That's to be expected. You've had a slight concussion. So long as you lie quietly it will be all right, and you can get around a little without hurting anything."

"That will be exciting," he grinned, or tried to grin, but his face was too drawn to do it successfully. "Anyway, I'll have plenty of time to think what a rotten failure I've made of everything . . . and to consider other matters." He was rather limp now, although still half sitting up. "It's all off with the settlers and my Lost Lake plan and . . ." he did not say it, but his mind thought it, and the girl, watching, read it aright. And that unspoken thought was worded. "It's good-bye to Valentine, too."

"Amen," said Crete, almost aloud.

"Eh? What's that?"

"Nothing, David. I was just thinking you're too pessimistic. Don't give up."

"Give up? Why shouldn't I? I'm not far removed from a common failure."

There seemed little more to say, or to do.

"Good-bye."

The door closed behind her.

"Good-bye, dear Failure . . ." she was on Fan-tan now, smiling through a mist of tears . . . "dear successful Failure."

CHAPTER XXVIII

THE TRIAL

Not since the settlers' meeting had the hard benches of the Grange Hall accommodated such an audience as gathered to witness the trial of David Kent, charged with the illegal destruction of property.

Seemingly everyone in and about Farewell knew the young Easterner had returned that morning from his mysterious trip, forthwith surrendering himself and demanding an immediate hearing before Justice of the Peace Asahel Brush, on the warrant issued for his arrest. If guilty, as charged, he would be bound over to the Grand Jury, under bond, and subsequently would undergo trial at the next session of the Circuit Court. If innocent —but no one conceived such a possibility.

"We've got the goods on him sure this time," growled Hartpool with satisfaction.

"It's a bygod shame, but it looks as if they'd cinch him," lamented Dad Trumble.

Thus it went throughout the improvised court room. Everyone was convinced of Kent's guilt . . . indeed, there was no logical possibility of

The Trial 305

feeling otherwise, for had not Pharaoh Jones admitted the identity of the nocturnal marauder who had wrecked the special edition of the *Pioneer?* And was not the editor himself to appear as a witness for the prosecution? So the company crowd was elated and Kent's settler friends regretfully pessimistic.

Wendall, the district attorney from Roundville, was on hand. Failing had seen to that, gloatingly determined to settle scores once and for all with the meddlesome Easterner. A fat fine or a few months in the county jail, he felt, would have a wholesomely discouraging effect. The wind, which had started out so ill, was blowing well for him at last. And with everything developing as he wished it, the big manager seemed all smiles and purring good nature as he whispered with the imported attorney.

Wendall, a hard-headed, catch-as-catch-can cow country prosecutor, wasted no time on preliminaries.

"Does the defendant demand a jury?" he asked, as soon as old Asahel had rapped for order.

The defendant did not, to the astonishment of everyone.

The problem of selecting a satisfactory jury had been the only fly in the ointment of Failing's oily satisfaction. He foresaw a fight there and had already prepared lists of "ineligibles" for Wendall's guidance and coached the prosecutor as to whom should be avoided. So when the prisoner waived his right for jury trial the manager's cup of content fairly brimmed over. Things certainly were coming his way. Thinking that, he passed an excellent cigar to Wendall and lit one himself.

There was another ripple of surprise when it became apparent that Kent had no attorney. Evidently he intended to handle his own case, and seeing that the wise ones who knew Wendall's abilities shook their heads sorrowfully.

"Why, is he a lawyer?" a rangy settler whispered hoarsely in Dad Trumble's ear.

"Nary a bit!" growled that staunch friend in reply, his voice laden with anxious disapproval. "It's a plumb mistake, too. Dave's a bright lad, but he's no match for that bygod persecutor."

Dad's feelings were echoed throughout the hall. Even Crete wondered at these developments, regretfully; she expected that Kent would lose, but she also expected him to make a fight for freedom. But most curious of all was the aspect of Pharaoh, who seemed not the least cast down at Kent's apparent apathy; in truth, the usually somber editor appeared positively to twinkle with ill-suppressed gaiety and anticipation.

The prosecuting attorney stated the charge and outlined the main facts of the case, as alleged by the prosecution.

"Guilty or not guilty?" asked the justice of the peace.

Kent rose, then, with his boyish smile. But his face showed pale beneath the piratical looking bandage which cross-sectioned his head with a rakish halo. The wound had left him weak.

"Guilty as charged" . . . an audible and regretful sigh escaped the audience . . . "and *not guilty of any crime!*"

Wendall was on his feet in a flash.

"I object!" he shouted, scenting a play for sympathy. "Your Honor, the defendant can't plead both guilty and not guilty . . . it's impossible . . . there's no authority in law for it. . . ."

"And there's no authority anywhere for arresting an innocent man," shot back Kent.

"Innocent?" The prosecutor was politely facetious. "You just plead guilty. Your Honor," he turned to Asahel with a depreciating shrug, "there's no use wasting the court's valuable time with this foolishness. . . . I suggest the young gentleman secures an attorney familiar with legal procedure to represent him."

"One lawyer in the room is all I can stand," the prisoner retorted grinning impertinently, and a gust of approving titters swept the benches.

Old Asahel pounded the hammer which did duty as a gavel; the feeling of authority was reassuring.

"Guilty or not guilty?" He took refuge in repetition.

"I'm guilty of wrecking the forms in the print shop. . . . I did that all right, only . . ."

"I object!" roared Wendall again. "He pleads guilty. There's nothing else to it . . . no 'if's' and 'and's' about it."

"Exactly," breathed Failing.

"Oh, aren't there?" Kent's eyes flashed this time. "And who imported you?"

"As district attorney it's my duty," replied Wendall with dignity, "to prosecute malefactors."

"Fair enough! But I'm not a malefactor and just remember that before we get through you'll be prosecuting someone else."

However, the informality of these proceedings were here interrupted by Asahel, and the trial got under way. Kent, seeing it all was regular and unavoidable and with next to no ideas himself about legal maneuvering, subsided temporarily, with an amused expression disconcerting to the prosecutor every time his eyes encountered the prisoner's.

First came Failing, who told of stumbling over the editor in the shop where he had fainted after discovering the wreckage. He also described finding the envelope addressed to Kent and gave further information tending to establish the prisoner's hostility to the Bonanza Irrigation Company.

Through this recital the accused sat in bored apathy, but at the end of it, when Wendall was on the point of calling another witness, he roused himself.

"I object!" His excellent imitation of the prosecutor brought a smile. "As my own attorney I've a right to do that, haven't I?"

With elaborate deference he turned to Wendall, who nodded sourly.

"Well, your Honor, I'm like the district attorney here . . . I object to wasting time. There's no good reason to drag this out all afternoon . . . lawyers don't even get paid by the hour, I'm advised. If it isn't enough for me to plead guilty why not call Pharaoh Jones and be done with it . . . he'll swear I did it . . . he saw me. I've no witnesses to call . . . only a little statement to make when my legal friend over there has shot his wad."

But again it appeared that Kent was out of order. His plea could come at the last, after such cross examination as he cared to make. And in the meantime Wendall proceeded with examination of his witnesses. It was perfunctory and hurried, however, for now he was entirely certain that the case was won and the prisoner convicted; anything else was palpably impossible. Crete, Pharaoh, Miranda, and Frost, the stable man, all contributed their damning quota. Miss Pennoyer alone was absent. The only possible flaw was the non-appearance of that envelope addressed to Kent which Failing said he had found.

"Now, Asahel—that is, your Honor," Kent rose when the testimony was all heard and Wendall had refastened the guilt upon him with logical and scathing completeness, winding up with the demand that he be bound over to the Grand Jury. "Is it in order for me to . . . ahem . . . say a few well-chosen words?"

The J. P. nodded. But he knew it could make

no difference; there was nothing for him to do but sustain the charge.

"Thanks. I'm no attorney, as my friend has insinuated, but I'll try to make a sort of plea. Perhaps throwing myself on the mercy of the court is the legal way to put it . . . anyhow, it's by way of setting forth an extenuating circumstance."

Failing was smiling at him in an insulting, mocking way, and he saw it.

"First, I desire to put a question to the honorable district attorney."

Wendall, with a patronizing smirk, signified his willingness to answer.

"Is it a crime for a man to destroy his own property?"

"What's that?"

"A simple question." The prisoner cleared his throat, smiling sweetly. "Suppose I own a building and I take a notion to wreck its contents, every bit of which belongs to me—would that be illegal?"

"Certainly not!" the attorney snapped contemptuously, not in the least foreseeing what would follow.

"Well then, your Honor and friends of Farewell" . . . he turned to the audience, and especially to James Failing . . . "it's exactly as I tried to say at the start when they choked me off. I did just as they said I did—broke up those forms in the *Pioneer* shop . . . only it wasn't illegal . . . *because I own the Pioneer!*"

"Jumpin' Jemima!" Dad Trumble first broke

the silence, his delighted whoop echoing like an Apache yell. "If that ain't the bygodest..."

But the observation was swallowed in the deluge of cheers, handclapping, and hoots which rocked the hall as comprehension of Kent's statement spread.

Before the first joyous uproar had subsided the prisoner himself was thrusting into the hands of the district attorney documentary proof of his ownership, in the shape of a bill of sale duly signed by Pharaoh and dated the day of the alleged crime.

"And here," chortled Pharaoh, "is the check he gave me that morning."

As Wendall, amazed and disgusted, mechanically fingered these proofs positive, James Failing elbowed into the group, his eyes red with anger.

"It's a bogus sale . . . a forgery," he sputtered. "No money passed . . . don't you see, it's just a fake framed up to clear him?"

"Your trouble, Failing, is you've gone lame above the shoulders," retorted Kent. "And you're a rotten loser. It wouldn't have mattered if Pharaoh never cashed my check. What counts is that he gave me the bill of sale, for value received, and you know it. I've been the legal owner of the *Pioneer* since noon that day and so far as you or your district attorney are concerned I could have hammered the whole works into a pulp that night and you couldn't do a thing to me. You didn't own that special edition. You were simply going to pay for it when delivered, and you never turned over a cent."

He laughed full in Failing's face, and it was not a pleasant boyish laugh.

"I just babied you along with this trial to show you up good and proper, and I think I've done it. You started out to 'get' me, Mr. Manager, and instead I reckon you've got yourself into a merry little mess. Probably the next legal work I undertake will be an action against someone for having me arrested without cause." He turned to the district attorney. "There's a case for damages, isn't there?"

Wendall was too old a hand to cry over spilled milk. So he grinned good-naturedly and nodded.

"I shouldn't be surprised, Mr. Kent. Anyway, I believe it's safer to be on your side than against you!"

CHAPTER XXIX

WELCOME WATER

"As trials go, that's an epic," observed Pharaoh as they made their triumphant exit.

"Short, sweet, and to the point, anyway," Kent agreed.

"But when you get right down to cases," continued the jubilant editor, "what's actually the most remarkable feature of the whole business is that I managed to keep mum so long—its the only real secret I ever had from Miranda."

"You'd better hurry and make up with her, then."

Despite his attempted jocularity the ex-prisoner and new owner of the *Pioneer* seemed dull and preoccupied. The altogether satisfying outcome of the trial, even, had left him inexplicably somber.

"You're looking a mite funeraly, Dave. If I'd put over what you've just done I'd be tickled to death." Pharaoh laid his hand on the young man's shoulder. "Nothing wrong, is there?"

Their feet had turned toward the river and they found themselves now on the lawn before the

Company House. Half consciously Kent noted the untidy brown covering of new-fallen needles littering the grass, realizing that the house itself was closed for the winter. That Valentine had gone he already knew, but the deserted barrenness of the place, where he had last seen the girl and where he had told her his plans only to have the confidence abused, depressed him further. The dull misery of those recollections started his head aching again and realizing anew how weak the wound and the shock of it had left him, he gladly rested upon the steps of the deserted porch.

"Yes, Fair, there's plenty wrong. I'm glad you urged me to come in to get that fool warrant out of the way before I went East—the trial was worth the trip. I'll never forget the look on Failing's face! That helped, all right, but taken all in all he is the one who comes out on top of the heap . . . I'm done."

"Goodness me! That sounds mournful." It was the quiet voice of Crete Colton.

"Anyway, congratulations!" she hurried on, happily. "Everyone but your friend Mr. Failing is talking about the trial—what he says can't be repeated! Really, you're a lot better lawyer than you are dynamiter."

He thanked her, and the smile which lit his face made it for the moment genuinely carefree.

"But tell me" . . . she glanced over her shoulder in mock apprehension . . . "did you really intend Pharaoh to cash that check . . . and are you going to become a law-abiding newspaper man?"

"That I refuse to answer . . . on advice of counsel."

"And being your own attorney of course it's good advice . . . at least, easy to take! Anyway, I'll not press the question, and like a good girl I'll run along now. . . . I'm going over to congratulate Miranda upon having such a discreet husband," she added, mischievously.

"Oh! goodness, please . . . that is . . ." the editor's words tangled. Above all things he wished to break the news to Miranda himself.

"You see the duplicity of the man!" David laughed. "He actually fears you'll make trouble for him with his wife. Pharaoh, take my advice and get to Miranda as quickly as you can. In the meanwhile I'll detain this telltale until you've had a chance to square yourself . . . that is, if she'll stay. Will you?"

"Oh, certainly," answered Crete.

When the lean figure of the editor had shuffled off across the lawn beyond earshot, the girl, settling herself on the steps below David, said to him, without turning her head:

"Quitting again?"

Silence for a moment. He recalled how once before she had encountered him on the point of abandoning Farewell. That time he wavered only momentarily. But now everything was different. There was no incentive to push on. Before, he had expected to win Valentine over, at least to a realization of the justice of the settlers' cause; and now Valentine was gone, contemptuous of Farewell and of himself. Before, he was buoyed up by the hopeful expectation of solving all the irrigation problems through his plan for capturing the waters of Lost Lake, a remedy overlooked by the engineers themselves with the unimaginative narrowness so often typical of technical men; and now, thanks to a blizzard, a warrant, and a dynamite-thrown rock, his scheme had come to melodramatic ruin. Failing, no doubt, was already in possession of those water rights . . . had them, indeed, because the girl for whom he undertook it all had betrayed him.

"Quitting again?" This other girl's question sounded in his ear, as he gazed forlornly out over the gray water of Welcome River that chill October afternoon.

"No, not again . . . still."

He tried to be jocular, succeeding miserably. Then he recalled that on that other occasion, at the *Pioneer* office, when Crete had reproached his ebbing resolution, she herself had finally announced her intention of quitting Farewell.

"Why so sad, David? Now that it's all over . . . that awful time up in the mountains, I'm so" . . . she faltered . . . "so *happy*." Despite the wistfulness of her voice the whole look and spirit of her was radiant. "And it's so good to get back to Farewell. . . . Of course, if what you are go-

Welcome Water 317

ing to do is a secret . . ." she sighed whimsically and stopped, her eyes, too, studying the steely-cold waters swirling so steadily on their everlasting way.

Secret? An unreasonable desire surged within him to blurt out that he could have no secrets from her. Memories of the ranger cabin smote him sweetly, and fresh realization of his heart's awakening there. But all that was over. He was determined to put that behind him. . . .

"It's no secret, Crete." He found his voice, but it was lifeless and dull. "It's just that I'm through. I'm going back East . . . there's nothing to stay for now."

She caught her breath at that and all the gladness left her. "Nothing to stay for now." What a phrase! Each word cut into her heart and her happiness as her lips soundlessly repeated them. She had hoped—oh, how wildly she had dared hope! And how foolishly. Valentine was gone . . . gone to that "Back East" where David was now to follow. . . . And that, a cool, comfortless voice within her argued, was to be expected. Curiously little resentment embittered this subconscious realization; there was no effort, for instance, to justify David's protestations at the cabin that the other girl meant nothing further to him. The deep sad hurt of it all was glossed over, at least, by the good unselfish generosity of her spirit.

But what was the man saying? What, at least, was he trying to say, for the words came painfully slow, weighted with their own inadequacy to express the intangible things within him.

"It's hard to quit . . . to leave Farewell." The words dragged out of him in colorless procession, as if he were arguing, sullenly, with himself. His body was sick and weary and his hope and enthusiasm dead. "I came here for a purpose . . . you know about that . . . rainbow chasing, I suppose. And just as I had my hands on the pot of gold it all melted away . . . at least" . . . he realized that was not the truth of it . . . "at least I found that instead of the expected gold it was only dross . . . and I didn't want it."

She drew in her breath there, sharply. But the square little shoulders and the crown of dusty hair remained firm and motionless.

"It's all just as I tried to say to you in the cabin that morning when . . . when the blinders fell from my eyes. I didn't care and I really never cared for . . . for . . . well, there's no need for names. That's all over. But I had somehow come to care tremendously about this fight here at Farewell, and the way out of it all . . . the way to justice and happiness for these poor people seemed so easy . . . so attainable . . ." He paused there, rubbing his brow as one banishes memories of unpleasant dreams. "It's just that I didn't quite make good, Crete. So I'm quitting, as you are quitting, too."

"I'm quitting too?" She echoed the words wonderingly. "Why, what do you mean?"

He looked down on her, hungering to lay his hands upon the dusty hair.

"You told us you'd accepted that teaching job in Seattle. I supposed" . . . some new thought roused him there . . . "I supposed you were leaving Farewell. . . . *Aren't you?*"

Had the girl turned to give her answer she would have seen, and perhaps comprehended, the sudden light which transformed the pale features of the young man who was leaving Farewell.

But Crete did not turn. Instead, her eyes were very intent upon the leaden waters of Welcome River, and the point where they focused lay just at the water's edge on the opposite bank where a smooth, coiling eddy lapped the flank of a great, straight-sided stone rising sheer from the river's depths. The girl's attention, idly roaming, had unconsciously fastened upon this rock until suddenly the phenomenon of the water's steady rise along its surface roused her. At first she suspected her eyes of playing a trick, and she rubbed them and fixed her gaze with redoubled concentration upon the telltale rock. . . . Assuredly there was no illusion; the surface of Welcome River was steadily rising. She focused hard upon a tuft of moss which showed exactly at the water's edge, and as she looked the moss disappeared. In like manner a dark crack, which had been several inches above the surface, slowly was swallowed.

"*David! Look!*"

She pointed, but he did not comprehend.

"Don't you see? . . . *The river is rising.*"

Even then he did not grasp the meaning of it, until she had shown him how, inch by inch, old Welcome River, whose flow had never been known to vary, was suddenly and mysteriously gathering volume.

"It's Lost Lake! The outlet you dammed with your avalanche has backed up and overflowed to the east, just as you said it would. It must have taken days to fill the lake to the new level and a long time, too, for the water to find its way down the old stream bed to Little Lake and Welcome River . . . and it's just got here . . . *just in time to welcome you back.*"

Crete was almost hysterical with joy. She laughed and cried all at the same time, while the man wondered at her. He could not understand.

Nor could the girl comprehend him. The coming of that water from Lost Lake, a thing of his own accomplishment, seemed to mean nothing to him. He appeared almost sullenly indifferent.

"Why, David" . . . the happy tears adorably became her . . . "your plan worked. It's the key to it all . . . and we win!"

"We win?" he repeated numbly.

"Just exactly that." She wanted to kiss him, he looked so dejected—and for other reasons. "There'll be enough water now for the South Canal segregation."

"Yep." He was blunt, almost savage. "That's

Welcome Water 321

fine for Failing. I hope to God it helps the settlers."

"But David . . ." she paused, open mouthed.

All at once she understood. He did not know! He had not even guessed the accomplishment which made her so happy and so sure of success! As that realization dawned, her happiness surged up with a consuming flame which lit her cheeks and made her heart sing. He did not know; he thought himself beaten. And it was for her to tell him, to explain that defeat was really victory.

"But David, it isn't Failing's. Your filing on the overflow of Lost Lake has been accepted . . . *it's yours*. Oh! David, don't you see what a glorious success your plan has been and . . . and . . ." she dared not end that sentence.

"*My . . . filing . . . has . . . been . . . accepted?*" he gasped. "How . . . what the dev— say, Crete, don't joke with me." He was stern, even in his bewilderment. "Why, I didn't even make a filing."

"Of course you didn't!" The girl laughed outright at his puzzled expression. "I did the filing for you."

"You?"

"Yes. Little me. After leaving you at the cabin I made up my mind it simply wouldn't do to let you lose out . . . you seemed so pathetically down on your luck . . . it must have been pity." Her eyes twinkled. "Also, I'd a little plan of my own which your resurrection had sidetracked. So

Fantan and I hurried through to the railroad. Things came out beautifully . . . I just caught the morning train."

"Good Lord! You don't mean to say you rode all night?"

"Of course. At that we had exactly twenty minutes to spare for the seven o'clock train to Salem. It wasn't so bad," she reassured him lightly. "Whenever I was nearly ready to fag out something would make me think about the Sorensons when their crops burned up for lack of water last summer, or I'd see Callier making his filing just ahead of me . . . and that would brace me up and we'd keep on plugging along that endless old trail."

As she recounted her experiences, Kent, too, summoned up a mental picture. He could see the weary girl urging on the little horse through the black night, with the rain beating down upon them and the inky shadows of the fir trees engulfing them as they wallowed through mudholes and made stumbling detours around fallen logs, while the dank underbrush slapped in their faces, soaking with pent-up moisture. And he thought, also, of what preceded this experience. Of the hardships and strain she had undergone; of the heart-breaking struggle when she dragged him from the path of the landslide; of the foot-sore weary way down to the cabin; and of the midnight operation, when she sewed up his wound. And on top of all that, while he himself lay there in the cabin in the comfort she had provided, miserably abandoning the battle, this self-contained, steady-eyed girl had set out alone to snatch victory from defeat.

She told him, then, the details of that venturesome journey down the long stretches of the Ringo Trail and of how she had found the rangers who subsequently brought him out to the railroad, whence he went to Portland and later, at Pharaoh's urging, to Farewell. And as Crete progressed with her story, proud and happy to tell it, the grayness of the waning afternoon seemed to lighten.

"At Salem," she wound up, "I intended to make my own filing, thinking that no one but the person who did the actual posting of the notice at the water right location could file. But they told me that isn't true. If there is an affidavit by someone who actually saw the posting done they'll accept the filing of an absentee. As I saw you post your notice I made the necessary affidavit, and your own filing, giving one David Kent the exclusive control of the overflow of Lost Lake, was received and receipted for. And here's the receipt."

A little out of breath she stopped to fumble in her skirt pocket for the precious paper. Holding it out to David she added, with a malicious twinkle: "And if you're going back East please turn it over to me . . . *I* intend to stick by Farewell and fight things out to a finish."

"What's that?" This seemed to astonish the young man even more than the news of the successful filing. "Why, you said you were going to Seattle."

"And I was going . . . only remember, women are forever changing their minds. The very minute I had that receipt and knew the company crowd was beaten, mine changed. To go now would be like leaving a play at the end of the second act. No sir! I want my money's worth."

"So you foresee a happy ending?" That took him back to himself. For the settlers, act three, as she put it, might well be Utopian, but for himself he could see no very joyous outcome.

"Why not? As Dad would say, the rest is simple as shooting fish. With that extra water in Welcome River, and the right to it exclusively yours, it's impossible for the company not to accept any terms you lay down."

"Yes, it could be worked out readily enough." But he said it wearily. "There wouldn't even need be any State investigation, for there's ample water now for all hands. No need to drag Pennoyer in . . ."

"But he doesn't know anything about it."

"Who . . ." A memory of what he had seen at the Horse Cave checked him there, and his spirits sank still further. Likely enough Pennoyer did not know about the crooked flowage report. But Failing did. And what of her and the manager? He had almost forgotten that.

"Crete." He sounded very far away. "Failing knows. He is in it all. Once . . . last summer, at the Horse Cave, I blundered on you . . . and him. I couldn't help hearing and seeing a little. I'm sorry. I couldn't understand. Crete" . . . he paused, seeking words to express the hunger that was in him . . . "you've awakened me as no one ever did before and . . . and, Crete, I love you . . . desperately. No, don't speak . . . perhaps I should not, but give me a chance. I understand . . . at least I try to. I'm not going to ask you again. I know what you may have thought that time, up at the ranger cabin . . . but it's all over there. She never cared for me . . . God knows how well she showed it! I've come to think that kind—the pampered butterflies—don't know what love and loyalty and . . ." he checked there, but his eyes showed his belief that the girl before him did understand these things as he would have them understood. "Crete, you know I'm sincere . . . you know that this time I know."

She sat ever so still on the step below him. Her head was low, now, and she was sobbing. But her heart was glad. She did know.

"If you really love someone else I'll . . . I'll never speak another word like this. If it's Failing . . ."

Then she saw, and the realization left her breathless. She wanted to cry out, to laugh.

"Shall I quit now, once and for all—just as I determined to do half an hour ago? That will make it easier for Failing." He was relentless.

She turned her face up to him, then, her eyes starry through their tears.

"No, no! Don't give up. Stay and make them do what's right. . . . I'll be *so proud*." At that she broke down, burying her head in her arm, so that the next words, wrung from the very depths of her, were scarcely audible.

"I hate Jim Failing! It was just . . . just loneliness and . . . and the bigness of him. I guess I was flattered and let him make love to me . . . a little. But that Sunday in the Cave . . . that was the only time . . . it ended there."

"You love someone else, then?" His voice was level, laden with torment.

"Yes . . . I love . . . someone else."

Why, why was he so blind?

The Bishop! In a flash the thought struck him. And why not? Where could there be a finer or a fitter man? Despite his heartache he was glad, or tried to be.

There was silence then, he looking out to the river with eyes that did not see, across the sturdy little shoulders and the golden dusty hair.

"I hope . . . I hope you'll stay . . . and help."

She said it carefully, as if she had thought out the words in advance, and dared not trust extemporizing.

He shook himself.

"I will." Wording that resolution seemed to lift a great weight from him. "I'll stay, if you will. Is it a bargain?" He was standing before her now, holding out his hand. "Shake."

Crete, seeing the look of renewed resolve, gloried in it. There was sweetness in knowing that she had kindled it, at least, even if he could not comprehend what was in her heart. And her right hand clasped his, manfully, sealing their bargain.

"Mother of Moses!" he ejaculated wonderingly, more to himself than aloud, and retaining that small, strong brown hand. "What a girl you are . . . and what a stupid fool I've been."

Then the man's fingers tightened and this time the tears were in his eyes as he looked down at her. And the question he asked seemed to her extraordinary beyond understanding.

"Are you certain you love the Bishop?"

What did he mean? Her mystification was complete. Amazed, she stared at him, wordless. And her hand still lay in his.

"What . . . what do you mean?" Finally she could speak.

"Just what I say." The lines of his face were drawn. "You said you didn't love Failing . . . but that you loved someone else."

"Well?" It was the merest whisper. He failed to see the sudden dancing light which suffused the blue eyes, because they were lowered.

"It sort of came over me that it must be the Bishop . . . and . . . and I'm glad for your sake because . . . he's a very fine fellow," he ended lamely, and tragically.

"David," she was making not the slightest effort to disengage her hand, and the blue eyes wavered up to his, "it wasn't the Bishop."

The dusty-golden crown swayed nearer him.

"It was . . . it is . . . ."

Crete never completed that sentence.

THE END

Check Out More Titles From HardPress Classics Series In this collection we are offering thousands of classic and hard to find books. This series spans a vast array of subjects — so you are bound to find something of interest to enjoy reading and learning about.

Subjects:
Architecture
Art
Biography & Autobiography
Body, Mind &Spirit
Children & Young Adult
Dramas
Education
Fiction
History
Language Arts & Disciplines
Law
Literary Collections
Music
Poetry
Psychology
Science
…and many more.

Visit us at www.hardpress.net

Im TheStory
personalised classic books

"Beautiful gift.. lovely finish. My Niece loves it, so precious!"

Helen R Brumfieldon

★★★★★

FOR KIDS, PARTNERS AND FRIENDS

Timeless books such as:

 Kids

Alice in Wonderland • The Jungle Book • The Wonderful Wizard of Oz
Peter and Wendy • Robin Hood • The Prince and The Pauper
The Railway Children • Treasure Island • A Christmas Carol

 Adults

Romeo and Juliet • Dracula

Highly Customizable • *Change* Books Title • *Replace* Characters Names with yours • *Upload* Photo Bar inside page) • *Add* Inscriptions

Visit ImTheStory.com
and order yours today!